T0408904

PETER SIDWELL'S

KITCHEN

100 DELICIOUS RECIPES TO
CHANGE THE WAY YOU COOK

We have enjoyed Peter's cooking many times and love his attention to detail, flavour combinations and sense of fun. His latest cookbook looks unbelievably good and is bursting with amazing recipes that definitely make us want to get cooking. It's great for all the family and perfect for foodies who love spending time in the kitchen. Our favourite recipes are the Homemade Hobnobs, Sourdough Bread, Curry Night, and the Epic Lasagne. This book is going to be well used in our kitchen.

- Amy and James Milner MBE, Premier League Footballer

Peter is a long-time friend of mine and he never ceases to amaze me in the kitchen. The way Peter has written his latest book is undoubtedly a triumph for a number of reasons: firstly, because it's accessible to everyone; secondly, because his recipes are easy to follow; and, thirdly, because it gives us ideas for developing our own recipes. From Bake it Better to Weekend Feasts to Four Ways With, Peter not only provides us with valuable information on how to create wonderful recipes, but he also inspires us as cooks - plus, his unique take on flapjacks will definitely get the children cooking! One of my favourite recipes has to be his Miso Glazed Salmon with Pickled Watermelon Salsa, and I can't wait to test this out myself.

- Rosemary Shrager, TV chef, presenter and author

So many inspiring recipes – many with a clever twist – plus photography so beautiful you want to lick the page! Top of my To-Make list are the Chorizo and Potato Tart and the Treacle Bread Muffins. Well done, Peter!

- Karen Barnes, award-winning editor and freelance writer.
Find Karen's food and travel newsletter, KB's Joyous Things, at substack.com

PETER SIDWELL'S

KITCHEN

©2024 Peter Sidwell &
Meze Publishing Limited
First edition printed in 2024 in the UK
ISBN: 978-1-915538-2-60
Written by: Peter Sidwell
Edited by: Emily Readman
Photography by: Emily Grey, Carlos Reina Silvestre
Designed by: Paul Cocker
Sales & Marketing: Emma Toogood
Printed and bound in the UK by
Bell & Bain Ltd, Glasgow

Published by Meze Publishing Limited
Unit 1b, 2 Kelham Square
Kelham Riverside
Sheffield S3 8SD
Web: www.mezepublishing.co.uk
Telephone: 0114 275 7709
Email: info@mezepublishing.co.uk

INTRODUCTION

Peter Sidwell's Kitchen has been 12 years in the making - that's how long it's been since I last wrote a book. Lots has happened in those 12 years, both in and out of the kitchen: children, dogs, and building houses to mention just a few.

During that time, I also launched my weekly cookery show, also Peter Sidwell's Kitchen. It was born out of lockdown back in 2020, when we were all stuck in our homes with not much to do but cook. I have been lucky enough to present several different TV shows over the years, but starting my own show meant I was finally able to just cook and chat to the viewer about my recipes, ideas, and techniques. With the show going from strength to strength, reaching audiences all around the world, I decided it was time to put pen to paper and create a cookbook: one that not only helped you recreate my recipes from the show, but that would inspire you in the kitchen and teach you the basic skills you need to start tweaking recipes yourself. Flavour is everything in my kitchen, so these recipes are focused on a solid foundation of technique that will allow you to combine flavours that just work together.

This book is very much a slice of what we all get up to as a family in the kitchen, both at home and at work. The recipes that follow are a collection of my all-time classics that I use at work, at home, and when I travel and cook in various locations, countries and at events. There are also lots of new and exciting recipes that I just had to share with you.

I get asked all the time for certain recipes, such as my Perfect Brownie (see page 28), my Blueberry and Pumpkin Seed Flapjack (see page 163), and my Miso Glazed Salmon (see page 114). There are, however, many brand-new recipes in the book that have evolved from the discovery of new ingredients. My team and I have really enjoyed crafting exciting recipes that work with everyday life. All the recipes here have been created, tested and enjoyed with the help of my dedicated team – who never fail to give me their honest opinion – so I'm sure you'll love them, too.

I hope this book inspires you to get into the kitchen and cook. My culinary style is all about flavour and ingredient-led cooking, meaning I often start with an ingredient that I want to cook or one that's at its best. I never walk into a supermarket thinking, "Right, what I am going to cook?" At the end of this book, I hope you feel the same.

Pete

A THANK YOU FROM PETER

I am unbelievably grateful to everyone who has supported this project and played a part in making Peter Sidwell's Kitchen a reality.

Our list of thanks is lengthy but incredibly important and, in no particular order, includes:

Symphony Group (www.symphony-group.co.uk/kitchens), whom I have had the pleasure of working with for well over ten years. I love spending time in my beautiful, custom kitchens, both at work and at home.

International Stones (www.istones.co.uk), for their support in taking my amazing studio kitchen and garden kitchen to the next level with their beautiful stone worktops.

AEG (www.aeg.co.uk/kitchen/cooking) – I am lucky enough to be able to cook on your appliances in both my studio and family kitchen. Every recipe in this book has been tried and tested with your help.

Masterclass (www.masterclass.co), distributed by **Lifetime Brands Europe** - my kitchen is full of your amazing equipment and they help me every day to create my recipes.

Beefsteak Club (www.beefsteakclubwines.com), for the pleasure of discovering and tasting your delicious wines while cooking all my recipes for this book. I'd highly recommend your excellent range of wines, many of which are available in local supermarkets and grocers.

Our publishers, **Meze Publishing** - a special thanks to Phil, Paul, Emma and Emily for bringing everything together.

To **Emily Grey** and **Carlos Reina**, who are my photographers and colleagues, but also my friends. I love hanging out with you in the studio kitchen, and I can't wait to see what the future holds for us as a team.

Finally, to my wife **Emma**, who puts up with me and all my ideas. You are my lobster. To **Poppy**, my daughter, who is growing up to become a beautiful and amazing young lady, and to **Thomas**, my son and best bud, whom I love spending time with, both on and off the football pitch (when he lets me).

CONTENTS

4 WAYS WITH...

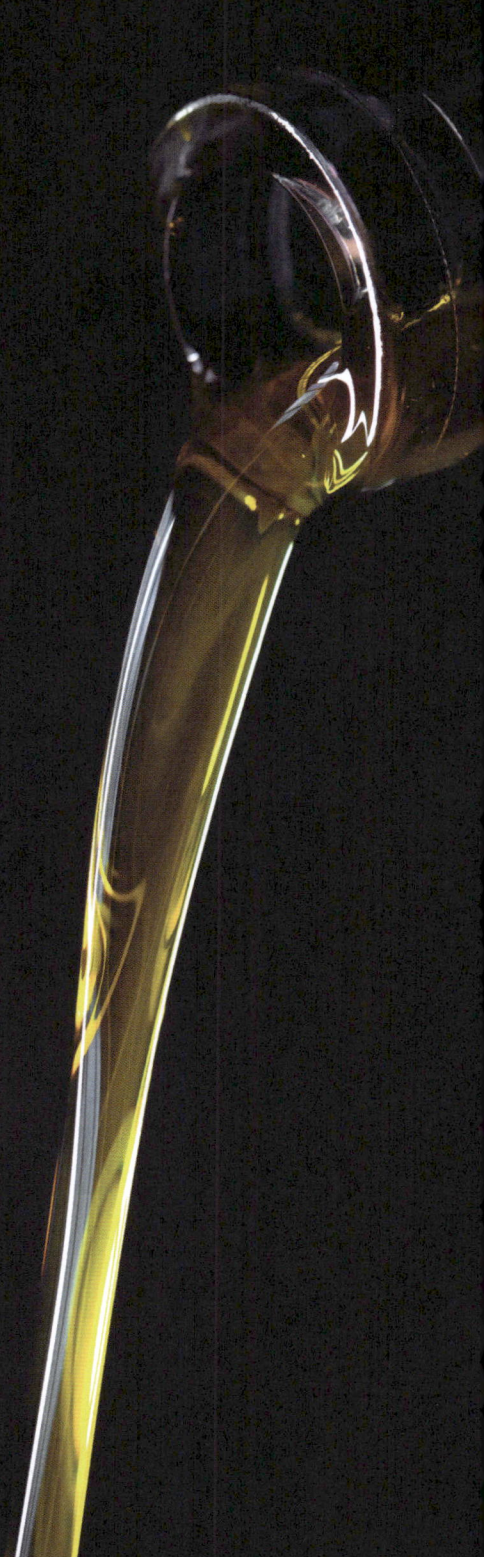

HI, I'M PETER SIDWELL ... WELCOME TO MY KITCHEN!

You've probably heard me say that a lot if you already watch my online show, Peter Sidwell's Kitchen, but if you're new, here's how we got here…

My cooking journey started back when I was a teenager. I'd always been a hard worker, with both a paper and milk round starting off my mornings, but I stepped into my first professional kitchen aged 14 when I got a job at the local pub. I was struggling a bit with school at the time and my mum was keen to keep me out of trouble, so spending my weekends cutting carrots and buttering bread for prawn cocktails was one way to avoid it. It wasn't the most exciting start, but from there I enrolled at Beverley Catering College (which also meant I avoided the army). While my dyslexia might have prevented me from acing the written work, it helped me flow in the kitchen - smelling, touching and tasting the ingredients was second nature to me. Getting stuck in was how I learnt best.

My first job in a proper serious kitchen was at the Ambassador Hotel in York, which is where I met one of my first mentors: Patrick Smith. I always say the four chefs you work with in your early years make up a quarter of you as a chef, and Patrick's influence has been the foundation of my learning. He took me under his wing and taught me all about food, ingredients, and cooking at a higher level. Having grown up with a sergeant major for a dad, I was no stranger to the militant feel of a serious kitchen, and I threw myself into it. From delis to markets, and England to Italy, I became fascinated by ingredients and what I could do with them.

But you quickly climb the ladder as a chef, and as I moved up in kitchens I soon realised it was time to become my own teacher. Aged 25, my wife Emma and I took a risk and sold everything we owned to move to the Lake District and set up our own café and deli, Good Taste. This was the inspiration for my self-published debut cookbook Simply Good Taste, full of all the recipes I loved cooking for our customers. Its 5,000-copy print run sold out in 6 months.

From there, things really started to take off. I managed to blag a TV deal with Channel 4, filming Lakes on a Plate around my new home, the Lake District. I was headhunted for ITV's Britain's Best Bakery alongside Mich Turner, and I secured a three-book deal with Simon & Schuster. Life got really busy really fast, and I was chuffed to be getting paid to do what I loved best - cooking, sharing recipes, and chatting to people about food.

After a while, and with two young kids in tow, stretching myself between our home in the Lakes, London TV studios, and our family business became a lot to juggle. At the end of the day, I wanted to cook and I wanted to be a proper dad to my kids. I realised I had to do something different in order to be there for them, so we sold the café and I set up work from home (way before it became the done thing). Cooking for me is a lifestyle, not a job, and I knew I needed something that worked with my life and family. When we built our family home back in 2020, I built a studio kitchen alongside our family one, and this became a creative hub for all my recipe testing. After a few years dabbling in live shows across the country, the Covid-19 pandemic hit, and through this adversity Peter Sidwell's Kitchen was born. It was the type of show I'd always wanted to make - ingredient-led cooking and a space where I could chat with my audience, kind of like I used to chat to my customers at the café, or to audience members in live demos. Just cooking, like most people do, day to day.

The kitchen is my happy place - no matter where on the map it is - and cooking has always come naturally to me. As much as I was taught technique and followed structure, I've always been led by taste, creativity, and intuition. The ingredients have always been my guide, not the recipe, and I've searched for new and exciting ones all across the world. From a couple of bottles of Poppy wine from California to a suitcase full of buffalo mozzarella from Campania (leave the clothes, take the cheese), I can't make it onto a plane without a taste of wherever I've just visited. Travel makes the best chefs, and we're lucky that the melting pot of the UK invites so many ambitious and parameter-breaking takes on flavour.

And that's exactly where my career has led me: to my online show and to this, an honest book of recipes that I've loved to create and love to cook. Recipes that come from innovation as well as tradition. The ones that inspire new flavour combinations and make people ask "How'd you come up with that?". In the UK, real home cooking is eclectic - it's Curry Night on a Tuesday, Epic Lasagna on a Friday, and Butternut Squash Soup on a cloudy weekend. There's no better feeling than enjoying home-cooked food with your friends and family (even when you're dealing with unbothered teenagers). I cook to make people happy - to get people excited - and I'll never tire of the smiles a simple Sunday sourdough can produce.

I hope you find that same excitement in these recipes. Enjoy!

Pete

TOP TIPS FOR MASTERING BAKING AT HOME

Baking at home can be a rewarding and therapeutic experience, allowing you to create delicious treats that satisfy both your palate and your belly. With over three decades of experience as a chef and baker, I've learnt a lot and mastered my own baking style. These top tips will help you elevate your baking game from the comfort of your home kitchen.

START WITH QUALITY INGREDIENTS

The foundation of any great bake begins with quality ingredients. Invest in high-quality flour, fresh butter, eggs, and other key ingredients to ensure the best possible results in your baked goods. Fresh ingredients not only taste better but also contribute to the overall texture and consistency of your creations.

PRECISION IN MEASUREMENT

Baking is a science, and precision is key. Invest in digital scales and always follow recipes closely, paying attention to exact measurements. Even a slight deviation can impact the outcome of your bake.

ROOM TEMPERATURE INGREDIENTS

Many baking recipes call for ingredients like butter, eggs, and milk to be at room temperature. Allowing these ingredients to come to room temperature before using them ensures better incorporation and distribution, resulting in lighter, fluffier textures in your baked goods.

MASTER THE BASICS

Before attempting complex recipes, focus on mastering the basics. Start with simple recipes like my Milk Bar Cookies (page 56), Nordic Bread (page 36), or Vanilla and Demerara Shortbreads (page 40), and gradually work your way up to more intricate pastries and cakes. Building a strong foundation of basic baking techniques will set you up for success.

PREHEAT THE OVEN

Always preheat the oven before baking to ensure even cooking and consistent results. Most recipes will specify the required oven temperature, so be sure to preheat accordingly.

MORE TOP TIPS

PATIENCE IS KEY

Baking requires patience and attention to detail. Avoid the temptation to rush through the process or take shortcuts, as this can compromise the quality of your baked goods. Take your time, follow each step carefully, and trust in the process.

PRACTICE MAKES PERFECT

Like any skill, baking improves with practice. Don't be discouraged by failed attempts or less-than-perfect results; it's not always about how it looks but about how it tastes. Use each baking experience as an opportunity to learn and improve.

KEEP IT SIMPLE

While it can be tempting to get creative in the kitchen, sometimes simplicity is best. Focus on combining the natural flavours of your ingredients and letting them shine through in your baking. A few high-quality ingredients combined with proper technique can create amazing results.

INVEST IN ESSENTIAL TOOLS

While you don't need a fully stocked professional kitchen to bake at home, having a few essential tools can make the process much smoother. Invest in a good quality mixer, baking pans and other basic baking equipment to set yourself up for success.

SHARE THE LOVE

Baking is not only about creating delicious treats but also about sharing them with others. Whether you're baking for your family, friends, or neighbours, sharing your creations is the best part of baking.

GIVE IT TIME

One of the best ingredients for baking bread is time, the more time you can give your bread baking, the better the results. Try proving your bread in the fridge overnight; the lower the temperature, the slower the prove, the deeper the flavour.

Bake It Better

BAKE IT BETTER

Many people know me as baker, so I wanted to create a collection of recipes that reflects my unique approach to baking. The success of baking very much relies upon the discipline of following the recipe, but once you've cracked that part, you can really get creative with the flavours – and that's exactly how I've approached this chapter.

MY PERFECT BROWNIE

Prep time: 30 minutes | Cooking time: 25 minutes | Makes 9

I've been baking this brownie recipe for many years now. As a chef, I've been lucky enough to travel the world cooking and baking, but this recipe has never let me down. It's always a crowd-pleaser!

INGREDIENTS:

185g dark chocolate (70% cocoa)

185g salted butter

100g caster sugar

175g dark soft brown sugar

3 large free-range eggs

40g cocoa powder

85g plain flour

100g milk chocolate, either chunks or buttons

1 tsp sea salt flakes

HERE'S HOW:

Place the dark chocolate and butter into a large glass bowl over a pan of simmering water and leave to slowly melt.

Meanwhile, whisk together the caster and brown sugar and the eggs until they double in size and are light and fluffy - it should take about 5 to 10 minutes.

When the chocolate and butter have melted, pour them into the beaten eggs and mix, being careful not to knock the air out.

Sift in the cocoa powder and flour, then use a metal spoon to fold it through, again being careful not to knock the air out.

Pour the brownie mix straight into a Masterclass square brownie tin (20cm x 20cm).

Sprinkle over the milk chocolate and scatter a little sea salt over the top of the brownie before baking.

Bake in a preheated oven at 170°c for approximately 20 to 25 minutes.

When ready, remove from the oven and leave to cool before slicing and serving.

 Scan the QR Code to watch how to make this recipe

SOURDOUGH AT HOME

Prep time: 24 hours, including an overnight prove | Cooking time: 50 minutes | Makes 1 loaf

Having a sourdough starter at home is the key to successful artisan baking. If you break it down into simple stages and work it into your routine, you will have the secret ingredient to AMAZING bread. Putting the time and effort into real bread may be a commitment, but it's worth it. The feeling I get when my family tuck into a fresh, warm sourdough loaf for breakfast is the best, and I want you to experience that too. My top tip would be to make two loaves: one for you and one for a gift.

INGREDIENTS:

FOR THE SOURDOUGH STARTER

50g strong bread flour

50ml water

Combine the flour and water in a jar.

Stir in 2 tbsp bread flour and 2 tbsp water daily over 8 days. When the mixture starts bubbling, it's ready to use. Keep refrigerated and feed with equal parts flour and water every week and again before making your bread to activate it.

FOR THE SOURDOUGH LOAF

Active sourdough starter (you will need 250g for this recipe)

400g strong white flour, plus an extra 20g to feed your starter before baking

310ml water

100g wholemeal or rye flour

150g mixed seeds

10g salt

 Scan the QR Code to watch how to make this recipe

HERE'S HOW:

Place 20g of strong white flour into your starter with 20ml of water and stir together. Leave the starter to activate for 30 minutes, then weigh 250g into a mixing bowl and add the remaining water. If the sourdough starter floats to the top, then the natural yeast in the starter is active and creating CO_2, so the bread will rise.

Add the remaining flour, seeds and salt to the bowl and, using your hands or a dough hook, mix until it forms a soft ball. Cover and leave to rest for 20 minutes.

Once rested, mix the dough for a further 5 minutes, cover, and leave to prove for 4 hours to slowly double in size. (This seems like a lot of work, but it's about creating a steady routine rather than being stuck in the kitchen all day.)

Once the dough has doubled in size, scoop it out and press the air out of the mixture. Then, holding the dough with one hand, gently pull the dough away from you and fold it towards yourself. Repeat this process, working your way around the dough to help strengthen your dough and develop a nice, open texture.

Turn the dough over and cradle it at 10 o'clock and 2 o'clock positions. Then, turn it in your hands to shape it into a nice, round loaf.

Line a mixing bowl, double the size of the dough, with a clean tea towel. Dust the towel with plenty of flour and place the dough on top. Put the dough into the fridge overnight for its final prove. (This slows down the fermentation process and develops the flavour.)

The next morning, preheat the oven to 220°c, or its max temperature. (I use a special setting on my AEG oven, which is perfect for baking bread.) Remove the dough from the fridge and lift it out of the bowl using the tea towel. Place it onto a baking tray and score the top using a sharp knife so it develops a good crust.

Put it into the oven and pour 100ml of water into the base of the oven, or in an oven tray placed at the bottom, to create steam, which in turn will help develop the classic sourdough crust. Bake the bread for 40 minutes or until golden brown.

Remove the loaf from the oven, carefully turn it upside down, and tap the base. A hollow sound means it's baked; a dull thud means it needs to return to the oven. If the latter, return it to the oven, reduce the heat to 180°c, and bake for a further 10 minutes.

BLUEBERRY AND HAZELNUT FRANGIPANE

Prep time: 40 minutes | Cooking time: 55 minutes | Serves 8

This recipe is based on a classic Bakewell tart, but I've gone rogue and used sweet blueberries and hazelnuts! It's the perfect pud to have after Sunday lunch with the family.

INGREDIENTS:

FOR THE PASTRY

250g plain flour

125g unsalted butter

50g caster sugar

1 lemon, zested

3-4 tbsp water

FOR THE FILLING

85g unsalted butter, softened

175g caster sugar

2 large free-range eggs

85g ground Oregon hazelnuts (or almonds)

95g self-raising flour

170g blueberry jam

125g fresh blueberries

60g roasted hazelnuts, roughly chopped

1 lemon, juiced

4 tbsp icing sugar

HERE'S HOW:

To make the pastry, place the flour and butter into a mixing bowl and rub together until it looks like a crumble. Then, add the sugar and lemon zest, and stir in the water. Mix to form a ball of dough, then transfer to a clean worktop and knead for 30 seconds to bring the pastry together. Place in the fridge to rest for 10 minutes before rolling out to approximately 0.5cm thick and using it to line a 25cm fluted tray tin. Place back in the fridge and rest for a further 10 minutes.

Once rested, remove from the fridge and place a sheet of baking parchment into the pastry case and cover with baking beans (or uncooked rice) and blind bake in the oven for 15 minutes at 170°c.

While the pastry case bakes, make the filling. First, beat the butter and sugar together for about 1 minute until light and fluffy. Add the eggs and continue to beat together, then stir in the ground nuts and flour.

After 15 minutes, remove the pastry case from the oven and lift off the parchment paper and baking beans. Carefully spread the blueberry jam on the base of the pastry, making sure to get it into all the edges. Then, spoon the frangipani mixture on top of the jam, using the back of a metal spoon to push the mixture around and cover the jam completely.

Scatter the blueberries and chopped hazelnuts over the top of the filling and press them down gently. Bake in the oven at 170°c for 30 to 40 minutes or until the filling is firm to the touch.

Once the frangipani is baked, remove from the oven. Mix the lemon juice and icing sugar and drizzle over the tart while it's still warm so it absorbs into the sponge top and adds a zingy touch. Allow to cool before serving.

HOMEMADE HOBNOB-STYLE BISCUITS

Prep time: 30 minutes, plus 1 hour cooling | Cooking time: 15 minutes | Makes 10

When I bought a packet of Hobnobs in the supermarket, I thought it would be great if I could make them myself. So, here's my recipe – I have to admit I think my biscuits blow the shop-bought ones out of the water. Once you've tried them, you won't go back.

INGREDIENTS:

125g self-raising flour
250g oats
125g granulated sugar
½ tsp bicarbonate of soda
250g unsalted butter
1 tbsp golden syrup
1 tbsp hot water
100g dark chocolate (70% cocoa)

HERE'S HOW:

Mix the flour, oats, sugar, and bicarb in a large mixing bowl.

Melt the butter, syrup and water together in a pan over low heat and bring to a boil. Pour the liquid into the dry ingredients and stir together until it forms a dough.

Portion the dough into ten balls of equal size and weight (about 70g - I do this by eye and then weigh them to double-check.)

Place the biscuit portions into the fridge and leave to cool for 1 hour.

Preheat the oven to 170°c and line a baking tray with baking parchment. Press the cooled biscuit portions down onto the tray before baking for 15 minutes.

When the biscuits have baked, remove from the oven and leave to cool.

Gently melt the chocolate until liquid, then spoon it over one half of each biscuit and leave to cool.

 Scan the QR Code to watch how to make this recipe

NORDIC SEED BREAD

Prep time: 15 minutes | Cooking time: 30 minutes | Makes 1 loaf

This is said to be one of the world's oldest bread recipes. Not only is this gluten-free, but it's also high in protein from the nuts and eggs. I bake this bread and cut it into small pieces for a snack - it goes great with my fat-free cream cheese recipe on page 60.

INGREDIENTS:

75g flax seeds
40g ground flax seeds
40g ground chia seeds
180g mixed nuts
5g salt
40ml olive oil
4 large free-range eggs

HERE'S HOW:

Preheat the oven to 160°c then mix the seeds, nuts, and salt together in a bowl.

Mix the oil and eggs in a jug before pouring over the nuts and seeds, then stir until it has combined and formed a sticky dough.

Line a 1lb loaf tin with baking parchment, then spoon the mixture into the tin and spread it out evenly.

Bake for 30 minutes or until the loaf is firm to the touch.

Leave the loaf to cool in the tin before turning out and slicing.

This bread will keep for 1 week and will freeze perfectly whole or sliced.

 Scan the QR Code to watch how to make this recipe

TREACLE BREAD

Prep time: 25 minutes, plus 3 hours proving (or overnight) | Cooking time: 1 hour | Makes 1 loaf

This bread recipe blends strong white flour and rye flour to make a fantastic loaf of bread. It's taken to the next level by incorporating the perfect combination of rich, dark treacle and crunchy walnuts.

INGREDIENTS:

400g strong white bread flour
100g rye flour
10g salt
7g dried yeast
2 tbsp treacle
300ml water
100g California walnuts

HERE'S HOW:

Place both the flours into a large bowl with the salt and yeast, then make a well in the middle and pour in the treacle and water.

Using one hand, mix it together to form a ball of dough, then transfer onto a lightly floured work surface and knead for 10 minutes until smooth, stretchy and easy to move about without sticking.

Return the dough to the bowl, cover, and leave to prove for 1 to 2 hours or in the fridge overnight.

When the dough has doubled in size, scoop it out onto a lightly floured work surface and knock the air out with your hands so that it's nice and even for the second and final prove.

Scatter the walnuts over the dough and knead for 1 minute to help evenly incorporate them into the bread. Then, shape the dough into an oval and place in a 2lb loaf tin.

Leave the bread to prove once again for 45 to 50 minutes, or until it doubles in size.

Preheat the oven to 180°c and bake on the middle shelf for 35 to 45 minutes or until golden.

To make sure the bread is fully baked, remove it from the oven and carefully slide it out of the loaf tin. Using a tea towel, turn the bread over and tap the underside. If it sounds hollow, it's baked; if you hear a dull thud then return it to the oven for a further 10 to 15 minutes.

VANILLA AND DEMERARA SHORTBREADS

Prep time: 15 minutes | Cooking time: 15 minutes | Makes 16

This simple failsafe shortbread recipe will serve you well like it has me for many, many years. I've stripped it back to just a vanilla shortbread to showcase the flavour of the final sprinkling of demerara sugar.

INGREDIENTS:

250g salted butter, room temperature
125g golden caster sugar
1 large free-range egg, separated (yolk for the shortbread; white for the outside)
1 tsp vanilla extract
350g plain flour
25g custard powder
70g demerara sugar

HERE'S HOW:

Place the butter and sugar into a bowl and beat with an electric whisk for about 2 to 3 minutes until smooth and combined.

Add the egg yolk and vanilla extract and continue to mix for 1 minute.

Sift in the flour and custard powder and mix gently with your hands until you have a crumble-like texture.

Tip the contents of the bowl out onto a clean work surface and use the warmth of your hands to press the mixture together and roll into a sausage shape, about 10cm in diameter.

Place the shortbread dough into the fridge to firm up for 10 minutes.

Meanwhile, preheat the oven to 160°c and pour the demerara sugar onto a dinner plate.

Once firm, use a pastry brush to coat the dough in the lightly beaten egg white, then roll the dough in the sugar. (The egg white will help the sugar stick to the shortbread, and when you bake you will get a lovely, sweet caramel crunch around the outside of the biscuit.)

Slice the shortbread dough into 1cm-thick portions and place on a nonstick baking tray or a tray lined with baking parchment. Bake for 10 to 12 minutes.

NOTES

This dough is great for keeping in the fridge or freezer for when you need it. You can also add chocolate chips, dried fruits, nuts and seeds - whatever takes your fancy.

Scan the QR Code to watch how to make this recipe

MARMITE CRACKERS

Prep time: 15 minutes, plus 1 hour chilling | Cooking time: 10 minutes | Makes 20

Marmite is my favourite ingredient of all time! Pairing it with cheese is a match made in heaven, so I thought why not put the two together and make the ultimate cracker? This recipe is bound to make you a Marmite lover.

INGREDIENTS:

115g butter, softened
225g extra sharp cheddar cheese, finely grated
1 large free-range egg yolk
2 tsp Marmite
150g plain flour
150g California walnuts

HERE'S HOW:

Beat the butter and cheddar cheese until smooth using an electric mixer on a medium speed. Add the egg yolk and Marmite and continue to mix.

Fold in the flour until just combined, followed by the walnuts. Gather into a dough then roll into a log shape and refrigerate for at least an hour, until firm.

Once the dough has chilled, cut it into 0.5cm slices and place onto a baking tray. Bake for 10 to 12 minutes in a preheated oven at 170°c until golden.

Cool completely on a wire rack before serving. These are great for cheese and biscuit boards or as a nibble with a glass of wine.

NOTES

Store any leftovers in an airtight container at room temperature for up to three days.

This dough will freeze perfectly, so you can also double up the recipe and save the extras for a rainy day.

Scan the QR Code to watch how to make this recipe

TREACLE BREAD MUFFINS

Prep time: 30 minutes, plus 1 hour 30 minutes proving | Cooking time: 25 minutes | Makes 9

English bread muffins: you gotta love them! Adding treacle gives these muffins a new depth of flavour that works so well toasted with a little butter and homemade marmalade. Don't forget to batch-bake these and store them in the freezer for a time-saving treat another day.

INGREDIENTS:

500g strong white bread flour
10g yeast
10g salt
310ml water
50g treacle
50g unsalted butter, melted
3 tbsp polenta or ground semolina

HERE'S HOW:

Pour the flour, yeast and salt into a large bowl and use your hand to combine the ingredients.

Make a well in the centre of the flour and pour in the water, treacle, and melted butter.

With your hand in a claw shape, roll it around the bowl to mix the ingredients until they come together to form a soft ball of dough.

Transfer the mixture to a lightly floured work surface and knead for 10 minutes until smooth and stretchy.

Return the dough to the bowl, cover, and leave to prove for 1 hour or until doubled in size. (You can also place the dough in the fridge overnight to prove, as the cold temperature of the fridge will slow the proving process down and develop the flavour.)

Scoop the dough back out of the mixing bowl and onto a lightly floured work surface. Dust the dough with a little flour on top and knock all the air out.

Roll the dough out to about 3cm thick and use a 9cm round cutter to cut out approximately nine muffins.

Scatter the polenta onto a tray and sit the muffins on top – this will stop them sticking – then leave them to prove until they double in size once more.

Preheat a heavy-bottomed pan on a medium heat, then place three of the muffins into the hot pan and cook for 3 to 4 minutes on each side or until golden.

When they've cooked on each side, place the muffins on a baking tray and repeat the process until you have cooked all nine muffins.

Bake the muffins in a preheated oven at 160°c for 15 minutes to cook through.

Serve toasted with butter and marmalade.

CHOCOLATE AND ORANGE SWISS ROLL

Prep time: 45 minutes, plus 2 hours cooling | Cooking time: 15 minutes | Serves 4

Everyone should be able to bake the perfect Swiss roll, and this recipe will help you do that. I've flavoured this recipe with chocolate and orange as it's my go-to favourite combination of flavours.

INGREDIENTS:

FOR THE CHOCOLATE ORANGE SPONGE

75g plain flour

25g cocoa powder

1 tsp baking powder

¼ tsp salt

4 large free-range eggs

2 clementines, zested (reserve the fruit for the cream)

100g granulated sugar

1 tsp vanilla extract

2 tbsp icing sugar, for dusting

FOR THE ORANGE CREAM FILLING

2 clementines

100g caster sugar

100ml water

250ml double cream

HERE'S HOW:

Preheat the oven to 180°c. Grease and line a 9x13-inch (23x33cm) baking sheet or Swiss roll tin, leaving a slight overhang of baking parchment on the shorter sides.

Sift the flour, cocoa powder, baking powder, and salt into a mixing bowl and set aside.

In a separate bowl, beat the eggs, clementine zest, and granulated sugar together using an electric or stand mixer until pale, thick, and doubled in volume. This should take about 5 to 7 minutes. Add the vanilla extract and combine.

Gently fold the sifted ingredients into the egg and sugar mixture in two or three batches, being careful not to deflate the mixture by stirring too much. Pour the batter onto the prepared baking sheet and use a spatula to spread it evenly to the edges.

Bake in the preheated oven for 12 to 15 minutes, or until the cake is springy to the touch.

While the cake is baking, lay out a clean kitchen towel and sprinkle it with a thin layer of icing sugar.

To make the filling, cut the clementines in half and place them in a pan with the sugar and water. Bring to the boil then turn down to a simmer for 10 minutes, until soft. Use a stick blender to blend the clementines until smooth, then pass through a sieve.

As soon as the cake is done baking, carefully turn it out onto the sugared kitchen towel. Gently peel off the parchment paper.

Starting from one of the shorter ends, roll the cake up tightly with the towel, and then leave it to cool for about an hour. This will help it hold its shape when you're ready to add the filling.

In a mixing bowl, beat the double cream until it thickens and forms soft peaks. Add the clementine purée and stir together.

Carefully unroll the chocolate roulade and remove the kitchen towel. Evenly spread the cream filling over the surface of the cake.

Gently roll the cake back up, starting from the same end as before, but without the towel this time.

Place the roulade on a serving platter with the seam side down, then chill in the refrigerator for at least an hour before serving.

LEMON ICED BUNS

Prep time: 1 hour, plus 2 hours proving | Cooking time: 20 minutes | Makes 12

This is nostalgia through and through. As a kid, we would visit the bakery and this would be the treat I would always pick. A perfectly baked, enriched dough, topped with a super-sweet, tangy icing… what more could you want?!

INGREDIENTS:

350g strong white bread flour

150g plain flour

14g dried yeast

1 tsp salt

1 tbsp granulated sugar

1 tbsp custard powder

325ml milk, warmed

50g unsalted butter, softened

FOR THE ICING

2 lemons, juiced

150g icing sugar

HERE'S HOW:

Combine both flours in a mixing bowl, followed by the yeast, salt, sugar and custard powder. Add the milk and mix with your hand to form a soft ball of dough.

Add the butter and combine before transferring the dough to a clean, lightly floured worktop and kneading for 5 to 10 minutes.

Place the dough back into the mixing bowl, cover with cling film, and leave to prove for 1 hour or until doubled in size.

Once the dough has proved, scoop it out and knock all the air out using your hands. Divide it into 12 equal portions and shape into bread rolls.

Place the rolls into a nonstick muffin tin and leave to double in size once more, then bake for 20 minutes in a preheated oven at 180°c.

When the buns are baked, remove from the oven and leave to cool for 20 minutes.

Mix the lemon juice and icing sugar together until smooth, then spoon over each bun. Allow the icing to set, and enjoy!

LAYERED COFFEE CAPPUCCINO CAKE

Prep time: 1 hour | Cooking time: 20 minutes | Serves 12

With layers of vanilla, coffee and chocolate cake all sandwiched together with silky smooth Italian meringue, this recipe makes for an amazing coffee cake like no other!

INGREDIENTS:

FOR THE CAKE
300g caster sugar

300g unsalted butter

5 large free-range eggs

1 tsp vanilla extract

300g self-raising flour

50ml espresso

1 tbsp cocoa powder

FOR THE ITALIAN MERINGUE
6 egg whites

350g caster sugar

8 tbsp water

HERE'S HOW:

Add the sugar and butter to a large mixing bowl and combine using an electric or stand mixer until pale and fluffy. Crack the eggs in one at a time, mixing in between each egg, until fully mixed. Then, stir in the vanilla extract.

Sift in the self-raising flour and gently fold into the wet mixture using a metal spoon so you don't knock any of the air out of the mixture (as this would result in a dense cake.) Once all the ingredients are combined, divide the batter evenly between three bowls.

Preheat the oven to 170°c and line three 20cm springform tins with parchment paper.

Add the espresso coffee to one of the bowls of batter and the cocoa powder to another. Fold the batter with a metal spoon until the coffee and cocoa are fully combined. Leave the third bowl as plain vanilla.

Pour each mixture into their own lined tin and place in the oven for 15 to 20 minutes or until firm to the touch or a skewer comes out clean. Allow to cool on a wire rack while you make the Italian meringue.

Place the egg whites into a clean bowl and whisk with an electric whisk until they form stiff peaks. (Make sure there's no grease or residue in the bowl as this will stop you getting stiff peaks.)

Add the sugar and water to a pan and place on a low to medium heat. Slowly swirl the pan until the sugar has dissolved. Then, turn up the heat and let the syrup bubble and boil until it reaches 120°c on a sugar thermometer.

Once the syrup has reached temperature, turn your whisk to a low speed so the boiling sugar doesn't hit you, and steadily pour the sugar syrup into the egg whites.

Once all the syrup has been added, turn the mixer to full speed and whisk until the outside of the bowl becomes room temperature, as it'll become really warm from the syrup. Once the bowl has cooled, the meringue is ready to be used to decorate the cake.

Place the chocolate sponge on a cake stand or plate and, using a palette knife, spread a thin, even layer of meringue across the top. Next, place the coffee cake layer on top and spread over some more meringue. Repeat the same process with the vanilla layer.

Cover the whole cake with the rest of the meringue, using the palette knife to add peaks to the meringue (these'll crisp up nicely).

Use a blowtorch to lightly cook the meringue, turning it a light to medium golden-brown colour. Keep the blowtorch about 15 to 20cm away from the meringue to avoid burning it.

HOMEMADE WAGON WHEELS

Prep time: 30 minutes, plus 1 hour 30 minutes chilling | Cooking time: 15 minutes | Makes 12

It's a blast from the past! Wagon Wheels were the ultimate treat when I was a boy. For this recipe, I've upped the quality of the ingredients to 70% dark chocolate to cut through the sweetness of the marshmallows and the jam.

INGREDIENTS:

FOR THE BISCUIT DOUGH
275g plain flour

1 tsp baking powder

100g unsalted butter, softened

100g granulated sugar

1 large free-range egg

1 tsp vanilla extract

2-3 tbsp milk (if needed)

FOR THE FILLING
150g marshmallows

2 tbsp water

200g raspberry or strawberry jam

FOR THE CHOCOLATE COATING
200g dark chocolate, chopped (70% cocoa)

30g vegetable oil

HERE'S HOW:

In a bowl, whisk together the flour and baking powder and set aside.

In a separate large bowl, cream together the softened butter and granulated sugar until light and fluffy. Add the egg and vanilla extract to the butter-sugar mixture and combine.

Gradually add the dry ingredients to the wet mixture and mix until the dough comes together. If the dough is too dry, add 2 to 3 tablespoons of milk as needed to achieve a soft and pliable consistency.

Shape the dough into a thick disc, wrap it in plastic wrap, and refrigerate for at least an hour to firm up.

Preheat the oven to 180°c and line a baking tray with parchment paper.

On a lightly floured surface, roll out the chilled dough to a thickness of about 5mm (a quarter inch). Then, using a round cookie cutter, cut out biscuit rounds. You'll need an even number of rounds for sandwiching.

Place the rounds onto the prepared baking sheet and bake for 10 to 12 minutes or until firm to the touch. Remove from the oven and let them cool completely on a wire rack.

While the biscuits are cooling, prepare the marshmallow filling. In a microwave-safe bowl, combine the marshmallows and water. Microwave in 10-second intervals, stirring in between, until the marshmallows have melted and are smooth.

Spread a teaspoon of jam on the flat side of one biscuit, then top with a spoonful of the marshmallow filling. Place another biscuit on top to create a sandwich. Repeat with the remaining biscuits.

Put a heatproof bowl over a pan of simmering water, then melt the dark chocolate and vegetable oil together, stirring until smooth and well combined.

Dip each biscuit sandwich into the melted chocolate, ensuring it is fully coated. Allow any excess chocolate to drip off, then place the coated biscuits onto a wire rack.

Let the chocolate set at room temperature or place the biscuits in the refrigerator to set faster.

Once the chocolate is firm, your homemade Wagon Wheels are ready to enjoy!

TEAR AND SHARE CINNAMON LOAF

Prep time: 45 minutes, plus 1 hour 50 minutes proving | Cooking time: 50 minutes | Makes 1 loaf

This recipe takes the classic cinnamon swirl and combines it with a classic brioche. It's layered with orange and cinnamon to make the perfect tear-and-share bread.

INGREDIENTS:

FOR THE BRIOCHE DOUGH
400g strong white bread flour
10g yeast
40g granulated sugar
30g custard powder
85g unsalted butter
9g salt
300ml milk

FOR THE FILLING
100g demerara sugar
1 orange, zested
2 tsp ground cinnamon
50g unsalted butter, melted

TO FINISH
1 large free-range egg, beaten
1 tbsp granulated sugar

HERE'S HOW:

Place all the brioche ingredients into a large mixing bowl and mix with your hands until they form a dough. Transfer to a clean work surface and knead until you have a soft, stretchy dough.

Return to the mixing bowl, cover, and leave to prove for 1 hour or until it has doubled in size.

Meanwhile mix the demerara sugar, orange zest and cinnamon in a small bowl.

Once proved, tip the dough out onto a clean worktop and roll it out to 1cm thick. Use a round pastry cutter (around 7-8cm) to cut out as many circles as you can.

Brush the circles with the melted butter and sprinkle over the orange and cinnamon sugar.

Place the circles of dough on top of each other in stacks of eight.

Then, transfer the stacks into a nonstick round baking tin, placing them horizontally around the edge of the tin. Repeat until they form a complete ring and the stacks support each other. Roll out any leftover dough to create more circles and fill in any gaps in the tin.

Leave to prove for 40 to 50 minutes or until doubled in size.

Brush with beaten egg and sprinkle with a little extra sugar before placing in a preheated oven at 170°c to bake for 45 to 50 minutes or until golden and fully cooked through.

Scan the QR Code to watch how to make this recipe

MILK BAR COOKIES

Prep time: 15 minutes, plus chilling overnight | Cooking time: 15 minutes | Makes 15

Milk Bar is a bakery in New York that places emotion and nostalgia at the centre of all its creations, so I've done the same with these Milk Bar-inspired cookies. I wanted to create a truly delicious cookie that made me travel back to my childhood. Adding ground-up corn flakes not only adds a nice texture, but also provides a comforting, familiar taste.

INGREDIENTS:

225g unsalted butter, room temperature
200g light soft brown sugar
80g granulated sugar
1 large free-range egg
½ tsp vanilla extract
250g bread flour
½ tsp baking powder
½ tsp bicarbonate soda
6g salt
270g corn flakes, crushed
125g dark chocolate chunks

HERE'S HOW:

Place the butter into a bowl with both sugars and beat together for 5 minutes.

Add the egg and vanilla, then continue to mix for a further 3 to 4 minutes. (I know it sounds like a long time, but it's important if you want to achieve an amazing cookie texture.)

Once fully mixed, it should be pale, light and fluffy. Add the bread flour, baking powder and bicarb, scatter in the salt, and mix slowly for 15 seconds.

Add the crushed corn flakes and chocolate chunks and mix again for about 20 seconds. This avoids over-developing the gluten, which will make the cookies dense.

Separate the dough into 70g portions and place on a tray in the fridge for at least 2 hours but ideally overnight.

When you're ready, preheat the oven to 175°c and bake the cookies for 11 to 13 minutes.

MISO CARAMEL SPONGE PUDDING

Prep time: 30 minutes | Cooking time: 30 minutes | Serves 8

Adding miso to caramel is a game-changer. I learnt this trick while cooking in California, and if you like salted caramel you're going to love this even more. Miso is a fermented paste that's sometimes used instead of salt. I know it sounds a bit unusual, but I promise you that it's the perfect ingredient for this recipe.

INGREDIENTS:

FOR THE SPONGE

140g self-raising flour

100g light soft brown sugar

1 large free-range egg, beaten

125ml milk

60g salted butter, melted

1 tbsp golden syrup

1 tsp vanilla extract

FOR THE MISO CARAMEL SAUCE

100g light soft brown sugar

2 tbsp golden syrup

2 tsp miso paste

300ml boiling water

HERE'S HOW:

Lightly grease a suitable pudding pan and place on a baking tray, then preheat the oven to 190°c.

In a large bowl, sift the flour and sugar and set aside.

In a separate bowl, add the beaten egg, milk, melted butter, syrup and vanilla, and whisk together.

Add the wet mix to the dry, and whisk until well combined, smooth, and free of any lumps. Pour the batter into the pudding pan.

To make the sauce, stir the sugar, golden syrup, miso and boiling water together until the sugar and syrup have fully dissolved.

Using the back of a spoon as a guide, slowly pour the sauce onto the batter. Then, place the tin in the oven and bake for 30 minutes.

Remove from the oven and leave for a couple of minutes to cool as the sauce will be very hot. Just like magic, the sauce will be on the bottom of the pudding!

Serve with Chantilly cream, ice cream, or custard.

EASY BAGELS WITH FAT-FREE CREAM CHEESE

Prep time: 45 minutes, plus 2 hours proving (and overnight for the cream cheese) | Cooking time: 25 minutes | Makes 9

The clue is in the title: *easy* bagels. Baking your own bagels at home can seem like a daunting task, but I've made this recipe more suitable for home baking. I've also added a cracking little recipe for a healthier cream cheese; the perfect topping for your bagels!

INGREDIENTS:

FOR THE BAGELS
475g strong white bread flour
1 tbsp Ovaltine malt powder
7g dried yeast
10g salt
325ml water
1 large free-range egg, beaten
50g mixed seeds

FOR THE CREAM CHEESE
500g 0% Greek yoghurt
1 tbsp salt
1 clove of garlic, chopped
2 tbsp fresh chives, chopped

HERE'S HOW:

FOR THE BAGELS
Add the flour, malt powder, yeast, and salt into a mixing bowl, and use your hand to blend the ingredients together.

Make a well in the centre of the flour and pour in the water. Use your hand in a claw shape to roll it around the bowl, then mix until it forms a soft ball of dough.

Transfer the mixture onto a lightly floured work surface and knead for 10 minutes until smooth and stretchy.

Return the dough to the mixing bowl, cover and leave to prove for 1 hour or until it doubles in size. You can also place the dough in the fridge overnight to prove it, as the cold temperature of the fridge will slow the proving process down and help develop the flavour.

When ready, scoop the dough out of the mixing bowl onto a lightly floured work surface. Dust the top with a little flour and knock all the air out using your hands.

Roll the dough out to approximately 3cm thick and use a 9cm-wide cutter to cut out approximately nine circles. Using a 3cm cutter, cut out the centre of the dough to make a bagel shape, then transfer them onto a nonstick baking tray.

Brush the bagels with the beaten egg, then sprinkle with the mixed seeds. Leave the bagels to prove for another hour until they've doubled in size, then bake in a preheated oven at 200°c for 20 to 25 minutes, or until golden and fully baked.

FOR THE CREAM CHEESE
Mix the yoghurt and salt in a bowl. Place a sieve over a separate bowl and transfer the yoghurt mix to the sieve. Leave to drain for a few hours or overnight to create a lovely, thick, cream cheese texture. Once drained, add the chopped garlic and chives and mix well.

Serve smeared on your seeded bagels for a delicious lunchtime treat.

CHEESE AND POTATO FLATBREAD WITH NIGELLA SEEDS

Prep time: 25 minutes | Cooking time: 15 minutes | Serves 2

This recipe is all about comfort, but it's also a quick and easy one to make. The flatbread enrobes all the delicious flavours in its soft and cheesy centre.

INGREDIENTS:

80g strong white bread flour

¼ tsp salt

½ tsp dried onion

2 x 10g butter, melted (10g for the dough; 10g for cooking)

55g milk

1 baked potato (80-90g)

2 tbsp mayonnaise

100g cheddar cheese, grated

1 tsp nigella seeds

Salt and pepper, to taste

HERE'S HOW:

Preheat the oven to 170°c.

Place the flour into a mixing bowl with the salt, dried onion and 10g of melted butter. Add the milk and mix to form a dough.

Transfer to a lightly floured work surface and knead for 2 minutes. Then, place the dough into the fridge to rest for 10 minutes while you make the flatbread filling.

Peel the baked potato and mash it in a bowl. Add the mayonnaise, grated cheese, and nigella seeds before mixing. Season to taste with salt and pepper.

Bring the dough out of the fridge and roll it out into a circle the same size as your frying pan (I use a Masterclass crepe pan that is 24cm in diameter).

Place the potato filling in the centre of the rolled-out dough and press it down to approximately 2cm thick, leaving 3cm of spare dough around the edges. Lift the excess dough into the middle and squeeze together to seal in the filling. Dust with a little flour and flip the filled dough over.

Gently roll it out until it's 2 to 3cm thick and the same diameter as your frying pan.

Preheat the pan and add the remaining 10g of butter to ensure the flatbread does not stick (you could also use oil if you prefer).

Carefully lift the filled dough into the hot pan and cook for 3 to 4 minutes on each side or until golden and crisp.

Place in the oven for 10 minutes at 170°c to make sure it is melted in the middle.

Remove from the oven and leave to rest for 10 minutes before cutting up and serving with some pickled red onions for a super tangy contrast.

 Scan the QR Code to watch how to make this recipe

FLOURLESS CHOCOLATE CAKE

Prep time: 40 minutes, plus 40 minutes cooling | Cooking time: 40 minutes | Serves 8

By sheer nature, this rich and delicious chocolate cake is gluten-free as it doesn't require any flour. It bakes to create an indulgent fudgy centre and works beautifully with the caramel sauce.

INGREDIENTS:

FOR THE CAKE
200g dark chocolate (57% - 70% cocoa)
200g salted butter
3 large free-range eggs
175g light soft brown sugar
100g mascarpone or soft cheese
¼ tsp vanilla extract
100g ground Oregon hazelnuts or ground almonds
1 tbsp instant coffee powder
30g cocoa powder, plus extra to serve

FOR THE CARAMEL
150g golden caster sugar
30g unsalted butter
60ml double or heavy cream
2 tsp red miso paste

HERE'S HOW:

Preheat the oven to 160°c and line the base of a 20cm springform tin with baking parchment.

Melt the chocolate and butter in a bowl set over a pan of simmering water.

Meanwhile, tip the eggs and sugar into a second bowl and beat with an electric whisk for 4 to 5 minutes until thick and creamy. Add the mascarpone and vanilla and mix until combined.

Lightly fold in the melted chocolate until combined and even colour, then fold in the ground hazelnuts.

Sift in the instant coffee powder and cocoa powder, fold together to combine, then scrape the cake batter into the prepared tin.

Bake for 35 to 40 minutes until the cake is puffed up and has cracked on top.

Remove from the oven and leave to cool in the tin for 30 to 40 minutes – it will deflate as it cools a little.

Meanwhile, to make the caramel, simply combine all the ingredients in a shallow pan on medium heat.

Bring to the boil and continue to cook until the sugar has dissolved.

Leave to cool before serving with the chocolate cake.

CALIFORNIA PRUNE AND CINNAMON BUNS

Prep time: 45 minutes, plus 1 hour and 45 minutes proving | Cooking time: 25 minutes | Makes 12

These delicious buns have an added fruity flavour from the prunes that works really well with the cinnamon spice. This enriched bread dough is super versatile and can be used to make all kinds of sweet bakes, so if cinnamon is not your thing, you can experiment with other flavour combinations.

INGREDIENTS:

FOR THE DOUGH
500g strong white bread flour
10g dried yeast
10g salt
20g granulated sugar
25g custard powder
300ml milk
100g unsalted butter, softened

FOR THE CINNAMON
AND PRUNE PASTE
2 tbsp ground cinnamon
1 lemon, zested
100g California prunes
75g unsalted butter

TO FINISH
1 large free-range egg, beaten
1 tbsp granulated sugar

HERE'S HOW:

Preheat the oven to 180°c.

Combine the flour, yeast, salt, sugar and custard powder in a large mixing bowl. Add the milk and mix with your hand to form a soft ball of dough.

Add the butter and combine before transferring the dough to a clean, lightly floured worktop. Knead for 5 to 10 minutes.

Place the dough back into the mixing bowl, cover with cling film, and leave to prove for an hour or until doubled in size.

Meanwhile, make the cinnamon and prune paste by placing all the ingredients into a food processor and blending until smooth.

Once the dough has proved, scoop it out and knock all the air out using your hands. Dust it with a little flour and roll out into a rectangle approximately 50cm long by 20cm wide. Spread the cinnamon and prune paste mixture over half of the dough, lengthwise, to approximately 0.5cm thick.

Fold the dough over the prune mixture to seal it, then cut the folded dough into 2 to 3cm strips.

Once you've cut all the portions, take a strip of dough and wrap it around your hand until you have only 5cm left, then wrap the final piece crossways and tuck the end in to hold it together.

Place the wrapped-up dough onto a baking tray and repeat with each strip of dough until all the buns are ready.

Brush with a little beaten egg and sprinkle a pinch of granulated sugar over the top. Leave to prove for 45 minutes before baking for 20 to 25 minutes or until golden brown.

Dad's

Dinners

xxx

DAD'S DINNERS

This one's all about creating dishes that both me and my kids will enjoy. I wanted a set of recipes that not only tasted amazing but that shared some ideas, hints and tips for how to cook feel-good food that's lighter and better for you... but that still packs a flavour-punch at the same time!

BIG BOY MEATBALLS

Prep time: 15 minutes | Cooking time: 25 minutes | Serves 4-6

These meatballs are not just any meatballs: they are big boy meatballs! Poached in a beautiful red wine and tomato sauce and finished off with creamy ricotta, this recipe takes meatballs to the next level and is one of my absolute favourites.

INGREDIENTS:

400g minced beef
150g pork sausage meat
150g fresh breadcrumbs
100g parmesan, grated
200g ricotta
1 large free-range egg
2 cloves of garlic, chopped
1 tsp dried oregano
1 tsp salt
½ tsp black pepper
100ml red wine
1 x 400g tin of Italian chopped tomatoes, sieved
30g butter

HERE'S HOW:

Preheat the oven to 180°c.

In a large mixing bowl, combine the minced beef and pork sausage, then add the breadcrumbs, grated parmesan, half the ricotta, egg, chopped garlic, dried oregano, salt, and black pepper. Mix well to combine all the ingredients.

Divide the mixture into 12 portions and use wet hands to roll them into balls. Place in an ovenproof dish and pour in the wine and chopped tomatoes so that they sit in the bottom of the dish. The meatballs will brown on the top and poach underneath - the ultimate mega meatballs.

Place in the preheated oven but leave the baking dish uncovered (you want the tinned tomatoes to reduce to a thick sauce).

Bake for about 20 to 25 minutes, or until the meatballs are cooked through.

Once cooked, remove the meatballs from the oven, stir in the butter and dot the remaining ricotta around the sauce. Let the meatballs rest for a few minutes before serving with spaghetti or as a delicious sandwich filling.

 Scan the QR Code to watch how to make this recipe

FLATBREADS WITH RED PEPPER DIP AND THE ULTIMATE TZATZIKI

Prep time: 15 minutes | Cooking time: 10 minutes | Serves 4

Both these tzatziki and red pepper dips are a winner in my house. They're perfect for placing in the middle of the dinner table for everybody to tuck into with warm, soft flatbreads. Once you make these, you'll never go back to shop-bought ones again!

INGREDIENTS:

FOR THE FLATBREAD
350g self-raising flour, plus extra for dusting
1 tsp baking powder
1 tsp onion powder
½ tsp salt
Pinch of fresh black pepper
1 tsp fresh rosemary, chopped
350g natural yoghurt

FOR THE RED PEPPER DIP
1 x 450g jar of roasted red peppers (drained weight 350g)
1 clove of garlic
2 tbsp cumin seeds
2 tbsp sherry vinegar
6 tbsp extra-virgin olive oil
40g stale bread
Pinch of salt and pepper, to taste

FOR THE TZATZIKI
1 cucumber
500g Greek yoghurt
1-2 cloves of garlic, chopped
1 tbsp dried mint
Pinch of salt and pepper, to taste
1 tsp red wine vinegar
2 tbsp extra-virgin olive oil

HERE'S HOW:

FOR THE FLATBREAD
Put all the flatbread ingredients into a mixing bowl and stir together with a spoon, then get your hand in to bring together as a dough.
Tip the dough out onto a clean, lightly floured work surface and knead for 1 minute to bring it all together.
Divide the dough in half, then divide each half into six equal portions.
With your hands, pat and flatten the dough, then use a rolling pin to roll each piece into 10cm rounds.
Place a griddle pan on a high heat then, once hot, cook each flatbread for 1 to 2 minutes on each side.
Serve warm alongside the red pepper dip and tzatziki.

FOR THE RED PEPPER DIP
Place the drained peppers, garlic, cumin seeds, vinegar and olive oil into a blender.
Blend until smooth, then tear up the stale bread and add to the pepper mixture.
Blend again - it should thicken up and turn almost creamy from the bread.
Check for seasoning and add salt and pepper to taste.
Store in a clean jam jar in the fridge for up to 2 weeks.

FOR THE TZATZIKI
Cut the cucumber in half and slice down the middle lengthways.
Use a teaspoon to scrape out the seeds as they hold too much water and will thin out the yoghurt.
Then, slice the cucumber into matchsticks before dicing into smaller pieces.
Add the chopped cucumber to the yoghurt as well as the chopped garlic and dried mint.
Season with a little salt and pepper, then balance out the dip with a little red wine vinegar and a couple tablespoons of extra-virgin olive oil.
Mix until combined for a lovely refreshing dip.

CHICKEN AND TOMATO PARMA

Prep time: 15 minutes | Cooking time: 20 minutes | Serves 4

For my chicken Parma recipe, I've decided to make a lighter, crispier, more flavoursome recipe that tastes just like fresh food should. Topping the chicken with cherry tomatoes and fresh mozzarella makes it not only easy but full of flavour.

INGREDIENTS:

FOR THE CHICKEN
2 skinless and boneless chicken breasts (180g each)
100g plain flour
1 sea salt
½ tsp black pepper
3 large free-range eggs
30g parmesan, grated
180g panko breadcrumbs
30g butter
1 clove of garlic, crushed
1 sprig of thyme

FOR THE TOPPING
½ clove of garlic
1 tsp fresh thyme
250g cherry tomatoes
1 tsp balsamic vinegar (red or white wine vinegar also work well)
2 tbsp extra-virgin olive oil
1 handful of fresh basil
2 x 125g balls of fresh mozzarella, cut into slices

HERE'S HOW:

Trim any excess skin or fat from the chicken breasts, then cut in half horizontally to create four thinner cuts of meat.

Season the flour with salt and pepper and spread out on a plate, then add the eggs into a bowl (big enough to dip the chicken into) and beat them.

Mix the grated parmesan with the breadcrumbs and spread out onto a separate plate.

To coat the chicken, first dip it into the flour, making sure it's fully coated. Then, dip it into the egg mixture before laying the chicken on top of the breadcrumbs.

Using a clean, dry hand, coat the chicken in the parmesan breadcrumbs and place on a plate ready for frying. Repeat the process until you have coated all the chicken.

Heat a nonstick frying pan with a little olive oil and, when hot, place the chicken into the pan. Be careful not to over-fill the pan; do it in two batches if required.

Meanwhile, to make the topping, chop the garlic and thyme and place in a bowl.

Cut the cherry tomatoes into halves and quarters, then add them to the garlic and herbs.

Drizzle over a little balsamic vinegar, then finish with the extra-virgin olive oil and a handful of chopped fresh basil before mixing.

Turn the chicken over and cook the other side for 2 minutes, then add the butter, crushed garlic clove and thyme to the pan.

Carefully spoon the tomato mixture on top of each chicken breast, then add two slices of fresh mozzarella on top of the tomatoes. Season with a little salt and pepper and a drizzle of olive oil.

Sprinkle any remaining breadcrumbs on top of the mozzarella before grilling for 2 minutes or baking in the oven for 5 minutes at 180°c.

DAD'S NOT A POT NOODLE

Prep time: 15 minutes | Cooking time: 15 minutes | Serves 2

This one's for my teenage daughter who loves Pot Noodles. As a dad, I wanted to create a recipe that she'd love to eat and that would allow us to share a few special moments at the dinner table together. This recipe can easily be made vegetarian, or it's the perfect way to use up leftover roast chicken. It's packed with flavour and fresh ingredients and tastes amazing.

INGREDIENTS:

1 tbsp olive oil

1 tbsp curry powder

1 tsp turmeric

1 tsp cumin

1 onion, finely chopped

1 thumb of ginger, chopped

2 cloves of garlic, chopped

2 tbsp peanut butter

1 tsp honey

275ml chicken or vegetable stock

1 x 400ml tin of coconut milk

2 tbsp light soy sauce

100g dried noodles

1 spring onion, chopped

Fresh coriander, chopped, to serve

Leftover cooked chicken (optional)

1 lime, cut into wedges

HERE'S HOW:

Add the oil, curry powder, turmeric and cumin to a pan on a medium heat.

Stir with a wooden spoon for 1 minute to gently fry the spices and really bring out the flavours.

Add the chopped onion, ginger and garlic and continue to cook for a few minutes.

Stir in the peanut butter and honey before pouring in the stock, coconut milk and soy sauce.

Bring to a boil then turn the heat down and simmer for 10 to 15 minutes.

Meanwhile, place the noodles into a bowl and cover with boiling water.

Once the noodles have softened, drain and add to the sauce along with the chopped spring onion, coriander and leftover roast chicken.

Finish with a squeeze of fresh lime and serve.

Scan the QR Code to watch how to make this recipe

EPIC LASAGNE

Prep time: 10 minutes | Cooking time: 1 hour 25 minutes | Serves 4

In our house, Dad's lasagne is best! So, I thought I'd challenge myself to make a fabulous-tasting but healthier lasagne. I've looked at each element of the recipe and worked out ways to trim the fat, up the nutrition, and still deliver bags of flavour for the ultimate comfort dish.

INGREDIENTS:

FOR THE RAGU
1 tbsp olive oil
1 onion, chopped
1 carrot, peeled and chopped finely
2 celery sticks, chopped finely
2 cloves of garlic, chopped
Pinch of salt
250g lean minced beef
250g cooked puy or brown lentils
200ml red wine
1 x 400g tin of chopped tomatoes
1 tsp fresh rosemary, chopped
1 tsp fresh thyme, chopped
1 beef stock cube

FOR THE WHITE SAUCE
550ml skimmed milk
30g plain flour
1 tsp Dijon mustard
¼ fresh nutmeg, grated
75g light mature cheddar, grated
Pinch of salt and pepper, to taste

FOR THE LASAGNE
250g wholemeal lasagne sheets
75g light mature cheddar, grated

HERE'S HOW:

Place a large, shallow pan on a medium heat. Add a splash of olive oil, followed by the chopped onions, carrots, celery and garlic.

Season with a sprinkle of salt to draw the moisture from the vegetables and help cook them evenly. Fry for 5 to 10 minutes or until soft.

Push all the veggies to the sides of the pan with a spoon to expose the base, then add the minced beef but do not stir or move the beef.

Let the meat cook directly on the pan and gain some caramelisation for at least 5 minutes before stirring.

Scatter in the cooked lentils and pour in the red wine.

Add the chopped tomatoes, then fill the tin with water and add that to the pan as well.

Add the herbs, crumble in the stock cube, and bring to the boil before turning it down to a simmer.

Cook the sauce for 20 to 30 minutes until it has reduced and you have a nice ragu.

Meanwhile, to make the white sauce, heat the milk in a saucepan but be careful not to boil it. Then, whisk in the flour, mustard and nutmeg.

As the milk heats up, the sauce will begin to thicken, so keep stirring on a medium heat so it doesn't catch on the bottom and burn. Once thickened, add the grated cheddar and season with salt and pepper.

To assemble, lay some sheets of lasagne over the bottom of a dish. Add a layer of meat and a little white sauce. Repeat the layers, finishing with a layer of pasta covered in white sauce.

Sprinkle over the remaining grated cheese, then bake for 30 to 35 minutes, or until the pasta has cooked and it's golden and bubbling.

NOTES
The best way to check if the lasagne is baked is to take a butter knife and gently push it into the dish. If it is easy to push in then it is cooked, if not then return to the oven and bake for a further 10 minutes.

 Scan the QR Code to watch how to make this recipe

CHEESE TOASTIE WITH PICKLED BLACKBERRY CHILLI JAM

Prep time: 15 minutes | Cooking time: 20 minutes | Serves 4

This toastie or, as some call it, "grilled cheese", is the ultimate comfort food. The sweet, tangy notes of pickled blackberries are perfect with the heat of the chilli jam, creating a combination of flavours you will never forget. You'll be serving this jam with everything.

INGREDIENTS:

FOR THE JAM
150g blackberries (frozen or fresh)
100ml white wine vinegar
200g jar of chilli jam

FOR THE TOASTIE
300g mature cheddar cheese, grated
100g mozzarella, grated
2 large free-range egg yolks
1 tbsp Dijon mustard
8 slices of sourdough bread
80g salted butter

HERE'S HOW:

Place the blackberries and vinegar into a shallow frying pan. Bring to the boil, then turn down to a simmer for 2 minutes, but don't let the vinegar completely evaporate.

Add the jar of chilli jam and stir together, then use a stick blender to blend until smooth. Transfer to a clean jam jar and set aside (this will keep in the fridge for up to 4 weeks).

To make the toastie, combine the cheese in a mixing bowl, then add the egg yolks and mustard and mix well.

Butter the slices of bread and turn them over so they are butter side down. Then, divide the grated cheese mixture between four slices of bread, making sure you spread it right to the edges.

Spoon over some of the blackberry and chilli jam, then top with the remaining buttered bread to make a sandwich, making sure the butter is on the outside of the sandwich again.

Preheat a large nonstick frying pan on medium heat. Then, place the sandwiches into the pan and cook until golden and crispy on each side. You may need to do this in batches.

If you have any remaining cheese mixture, spread it on top and place the toasties in the oven to finish off.

Scan the QR Code to watch how to make this recipe

CRAB LINGUINI

Prep time: 5 minutes | Cooking time: 10 minutes | Serves 4

I love the simplicity of this dish. These ingredients just love being in the same pan together. The sweet flavour of crab works so well with the fresh basil, and combined with the perfectly al dente pasta, you'll have an amazingly light pasta dish.

INGREDIENTS:

350g linguini
2 tbsp olive oil
1 clove of garlic, chopped
150ml dry white wine
200g crab meat, cooked and picked
1 tbsp lemon juice
50g butter
12 large basil leaves, gently chopped
Pinch of salt and pepper, to taste
Parmesan, grated, to finish
Extra-virgin olive oil, to finish

HERE'S HOW:

Cook the linguini in plenty of salted boiling water for about 9 minutes, or until al dente.

Meanwhile, in a large frying pan, heat the olive oil over a medium heat. Add the garlic and cook for about 1 minute until fragrant.

Add a ladle of pasta water to the frying pan, then pour in the white wine and turn down to a simmer for 2 to 3 minutes to reduce the liquid slightly.

Add the crab meat to the pan and gently toss to coat it with the sauce. Cook for 1 to 2 minutes until the crab is heated through.

Stir in the lemon juice, butter, and chopped basil (this needs to be chopped gently as it bruises very easily and will turn bitter). Season with salt and pepper to taste, then mix well to combine the flavours.

Lift the cooked pasta out of the cooking water and add it straight into the frying pan with the crab sauce.

Toss everything together until the linguini is well coated and the ingredients are evenly distributed.

Sprinkle with grated parmesan and add a drizzle of extra-virgin olive oil.

 Scan the QR Code to watch how to make this recipe

SAUSAGE TRAYBAKE WITH SPICED MANGO CHUTNEY

Prep time: 20 minutes | Cooking time: 40 minutes | Serves 4

I love this recipe. It brings together lots of amazing ingredients on one tray - all you need to do is cook it! The secret is adding the mango chutney. The sweet, fruity chutney gently melts over the food to make it all sweet and sticky. This recipe is always a hit when it comes out of the oven.

INGREDIENTS:

8 lamb sausages

1 tbsp olive oil

Pinch of salt and pepper

2 tsp garam masala or curry powder

2 red onions, each cut into six

4 sweet potatoes, peeled and cut into wedges

2-3 cloves of garlic, crushed

1 red chilli, chopped

2 lemons, cut in half

3 tbsp mango chutney

1 tbsp nigella seeds

Fresh mint and coriander, to serve

HERE'S HOW:

Preheat the oven to 170°c.

Place the sausages onto a baking tray and drizzle with oil, then season with salt, pepper and curry powder or garam masala. Stir well to coat the sausages in the seasoning.

Add the red onion and sweet potatoes to the tray and mix. Scatter over the crushed garlic and red chilli, then place the lemons in, cut side up.

Drizzle with a little extra olive oil to help crisp up the veggies, then cook in the oven for 40 minutes or until cooked through.

Remove from the oven, add the mango chutney and nigella seeds, and carefully squeeze the juice from the roasted lemons into the pan.

Give the tray a good shake to allow the mango chutney to melt with the roasted lemon juice and spices for an amazing flavour.

Finish with fresh herbs for a light, fragrant touch to your amazing one-tray dinner.

 Scan the QR Code to watch how to make this recipe

CHORIZO AND POTATO TART

Prep time: 35 minutes | Cooking time: 40 minutes | Serves 4-6

This tart is made up of a delicious combination of potato, chorizo, and onions. It's a very Spanish-inspired recipe that brings together ingredients that work well together. By layering the filling vertically, you get some cracking crispy bits.

INGREDIENTS:

FOR THE PASTRY

375g plain flour
175g unsalted butter, cut into cubes
3-4 tbsp cold water

FOR THE FILLING

250g chorizo sausage, sliced thinly
500g potatoes, peeled and sliced thinly
1 clove of garlic, sliced
2 shallots, sliced thinly
100g Manchego cheese, grated
Pinch of salt and pepper, to taste
1 tsp fresh thyme
6 large free-range eggs
400ml milk
100ml double cream

HERE'S HOW:

To make the pastry, put the flour into a mixing bowl with the butter, and use your fingertips to rub the butter into the flour to create a crumble-like texture.

Add the cold water, a little at a time, and mix until it forms a dough. Add more water if needed, but not so much that the dough becomes sticky. Transfer the dough to a lightly floured work surface and knead for 1 minute until smooth. Place it in the fridge to rest for about 10 minutes.

Meanwhile, to make the filling, place the sliced chorizo, potato, garlic, shallots and grated cheese into a mixing bowl and season with a little salt, pepper, and the fresh thyme.

Combine the ingredients and set aside while you roll out the pastry. Remove the pastry from the fridge and place on a lightly floured work surface. Roll it out to about 0.5cm thick — it should be big enough to line a 25cm tart case and have a little extra hanging over the sides. (I use a Masterclass fluted Crusty Bake tin as it's perforated with holes to ensure a crisp pastry.)

Carefully press the pastry into the sides and corners of the tin, as you don't want it to stretch and cause leakage when the tart bakes.

Preheat the oven to 170°c, then arrange the chorizo and potato filling in the pastry case. (I like to do this vertically so that the top goes crispy during the bake, but you can also lay the slices horizontally.)

Next, pour the eggs, milk and cream into a large jug and whisk together. Transfer the pastry case onto a baking tray and trim the edges of the pastry.

Place the tart in the oven on the middle shelf, then pour the egg mixture into the tart case while it's in the oven. (I do it this way so it's less likely to spill.)

Bake the tart for 30 to 40 minutes or until the egg mixture has set and the pastry is golden.

Serve with a chopped tomato salad dressed in sherry vinegar and olive oil.

NOTES

Always look out for a perforated tin when baking tarts, as you won't have to blind bake the pastry before filling it.

GRAPEFRUIT AND APPLE CRUMBLE WITH WALNUTS

Prep time: 20 minutes | Cooking time: 40 minutes | Serves 4-6

An apple crumble is a thing of beauty; it's simple, comforting, and delicious. After working on flavour profiles, I discovered something that surprised even me! Adding grapefruit to the crumble brings out the flavour of the apple and makes this recipe even tastier.

INGREDIENTS:

1.2kg Bramley apples, peeled and cored

1 pink grapefruit

200g caster sugar

Pinch of salt

100g California walnuts

100g plain flour (or gluten-free, or rice flour)

100g rolled oats

100g unsalted butter

1 large free-range egg yolk

20g cornflour

½ tsp ground cinnamon

HERE'S HOW:

Preheat the oven to 170°c, then cut the apples into 0.5cm slices and peel, segment and cut the grapefruit.

Add half the sugar and the apples to a large, shallow pan and cook on a medium heat. Add a pinch of salt to help improve the flavour – I promise it works – before adding the grapefruit. Leave on a low heat to soften.

To make the crumble, break the California walnuts up in your hand and place them in a mixing bowl. Add the flour, oats and butter to the bowl along with the remaining sugar and mix with your hands to make a crumble. Finally, add the egg yolk and stir.

Mix the cornflour and ground cinnamon with a little water to make a thin paste. Then, when the apples have softened, stir the paste into the fruit. The apple mixture will thicken as you stir.

Remove from the heat and pour it into an ovenproof dish, then scatter the crumble mixture over the top of the apples and grapefruit.

Bake for 30 to 40 minutes until golden.

 Scan the QR Code to watch how to make this recipe

WILD GARLIC AND SAUSAGE ORECCHIETTE WITH CHILLI AND FENNEL

Prep time: 10 minutes | Cooking time: 10 minutes | Serves 4

The flavours in this simple pasta dish are based on a Tuscan salami called finocchiona which I absolutely love eating. Fennel, chilli and garlic are iconic ingredients in Tuscany, and it made sense to just bring them together in a saucepan to make this simple yet delicious dinner.

INGREDIENTS:

400g orecchiette pasta
6 sausages, skins removed
½ fennel bulb, chopped
1 tsp dried chilli flakes
Pinch of salt and pepper
30g butter
1 handful of wild garlic, chopped
70g parmesan, grated

HERE'S HOW:

Cook the pasta in a large pan of salted boiling water for 9 minutes. Make sure to reserve some of the pasta water for the sauce.

Meanwhile, heat a large frying pan and add the sausages, chopped fennel and chilli flakes. Cook on a medium heat and, while it cooks, use the back of a wooden spoon to break up the sausages. Season with salt and pepper.

Add the butter and 75ml of the pasta cooking water. Bring to the boil to reduce the liquid by half.

Add the chopped wild garlic and the drained, cooked pasta, then stir together and finish with grated parmesan.

NOTE:

If you can't find wild garlic, substitute for 3 chopped garlic cloves, and gently fry them off before adding the butter and pasta water.

CURRY NIGHT

Prep time: 20 minutes | Cooking time: 1 hour 30 minutes | Serves 4

Nowadays, a good curry seems like a bit of a treat. This simple recipe, however, takes the flavours of this classic dish and makes it easier, fresher and better for you. Make it my way, and you can enjoy a curry any night of the week!

INGREDIENTS:

FOR THE CHICKEN
1 whole chicken
2 tbsp olive oil
3 tbsp Indian Spice Mix (see page 176)

FOR THE CHUTNEY
1 red onion, finely chopped
1 lime, juiced
1 tbsp nigella seeds
1 jar of mango chutney
1 handful of fresh coriander leaves

FOR THE COUSCOUS
1 medium white onion, finely chopped
1 clove of garlic, chopped
Pinch of salt
1 tbsp olive oil
1 tsp Indian Spice Mix (see page 176)
100g California raisins
100g whole roasted Oregon hazelnuts
250g couscous (approximately 1 handful per person)
2 tbsp nigella seeds
3 handfuls of baby spinach
½ lemon

TO SERVE
1 lemon, cut into wedges
1 handful of fresh coriander, chopped

HERE'S HOW:

Preheat the oven to 170°c.

Using a sharp knife, score the chicken legs and thighs down to the bone. This will do two things: it will let the spices penetrate the chicken, but it will also help to speed up the cooking process.

Drizzle a little oil over the chicken, then sprinkle with 3 tablespoons of my Indian Spice Mix.

Rub the spices all over the chicken before placing it in a roasting tray and cooking for 1 hour and 30 minutes.

Meanwhile, to make the chutney, add all of the ingredients to a small bowl. Stir the pimped-up chutney until combined and set aside.

Finally, to make the couscous, add the chopped onion and garlic to a pan on a medium heat. Sprinkle with salt and a drizzle of oil, then add a teaspoon of the Indian Spice Mix and stir.

Pour in 100ml of water and boil to allow the onions to continue to cook without burning. Add in the raisins and nuts.

Measure out the couscous in handfuls and add them to the pan. Four handfuls for four people equals around 250g. Add enough boiling water to cover the couscous by 1cm, then switch off the heat.

Stir in the nigella seeds then put the lid on the pan and leave it for 20 minutes.

When all the moisture has soaked into the couscous, stir in the spinach and squeeze in the juice of half a lemon. Then, push the couscous up the sides of the pan to make a well in the middle.

Remove the chicken from the oven and use a pair of tongs to place it in the middle of the couscous.

Finish with some of the roasting juices, then serve with the chutney, lemon wedges and plenty of fresh coriander.

 Scan the QR Code to watch how to make this recipe

CHICKEN KEBAB

Prep time: 20 minutes, plus 2 hours marinating | Cooking time: 1 hour | Serves 4

A chicken kebab is probably the ultimate dad's dinner. With this recipe, I've captured the elements of a kebab and made it work for a home kitchen, so there's no need to order a takeaway. Lots of fresh flavours and you can eat it with your hands: what's not to love?

INGREDIENTS:

FOR THE MARINATED CHICKEN
3 tbsp 0% Greek yoghurt
4 cloves of garlic, minced
1 tbsp olive oil
1 tbsp white wine vinegar
1 lemon, juiced
1 tbsp dried oregano
2 tsp salt
1 tsp paprika
½ tsp black pepper
1kg skinless and boneless chicken thighs

TO SERVE
Flatbreads, warmed (see page 72)
Tzatziki
¼ red cabbage, thinly sliced
2 tbsp fresh flat leaf parsley, chopped
2 lemons, halved

HERE'S HOW:

In a small bowl, whisk together the marinade ingredients, then place the chicken thighs in a large resealable bag and pour over the marinade.

Seal the bag, then rub the outside of the bag to make sure the chicken is fully coated in the marinade. Place in the fridge for a minimum of 2 hours or overnight.

When ready to cook, preheat the oven to 180°c and line a 2lb loaf tin with parchment paper.

Layer the chicken in the loaf tin and press it down to compact it. Then, bake for 1 hour or until the internal temperature reads 75°c on a meat thermometer.

Remove the chicken from the oven and let it rest for 10 minutes before draining the juices.

Transfer the chicken to a cutting board and slice as needed.

Serve with warm flatbreads, tzatziki, red cabbage, and parsley, and finish with a squeeze of fresh lemon juice.

 Scan the QR Code to watch how to make this recipe

MARMITE HASH BROWNS WITH FRIED EGGS

Prep time: 15 minutes, plus 2 hours chilling | Cooking time: 1 hour 20 minutes | Serves 4

Marmite is one of my all-time favourite ingredients, and I'm always trying to find ways of working it into my cooking. This recipe was created in lockdown when I was cooking out on the barbecue with Kerry Irving, the kids, and the dogs.

INGREDIENTS:

4 baking potatoes

Pinch of salt and pepper, to taste

2 tsp cornflour

50g salted butter

2 tsp Marmite

4 large free-range eggs

Fresh black pepper, to serve

HERE'S HOW:

Place the potatoes into the oven at 160°c and bake for 1 hour until soft on the inside and crisp on the outside.

Chop the jacket potatoes into chunks and place in a mixing bowl. Season with salt and pepper, then add the cornflour before stirring together.

Spoon the potato mixture into a square nonstick baking tray. Press the potato down into the corners and smooth it out so it's level. Place in the fridge to chill for 2 hours or overnight.

When the hash brown mixture is firm and set, cut it into portions. Then, preheat a nonstick pan on a medium heat and cook each one in a little oil until golden on all sides.

Add the butter and Marmite to the pan and continue to cook until golden and crisp. Remove from the pan and set aside while you fry the eggs the way you like them.

Serve the eggs on top of the hash browns, finish with a twist of fresh black pepper, and enjoy.

 Scan the QR Code to watch how to make this recipe

CHICKEN KIEV PIE

Prep time: 40 minutes | Cooking time: 1 hour | Serves 4

Chicken kiev is one of my all-time favourite meals, so why not try and work it into a pie? A buttery crisp pastry filled with all the flavours of a cracking kiev and topped with crunchy breadcrumbs and parmesan.

INGREDIENTS:

5-6 skinless and boneless chicken thighs

2 tbsp extra-virgin olive oil

Salt and pepper, to taste

4 cloves of garlic, crushed

1 handful of flat leaf parsley

200ml dry white wine

180ml double cream

2 tbsp mini capers

1 tsp dried oregano

1 tsp dried tarragon,
or 1 tbsp fresh tarragon

FOR THE PASTRY

250g plain flour

125g unsalted butter or margarine

3 tbsp cold water

FOR THE TOPPING

125g panko breadcrumbs

50g parmesan

1 tbsp olive oil

HERE'S HOW:

Cut the chicken thighs into strips and place in a large, preheated frying pan with a splash of extra-virgin olive oil.

Season with salt and pepper and cook the chicken until golden. Then, add the garlic, parsley, and white wine and boil until the liquid reduces by half.

Add the double cream and simmer for 10 to 15 minutes to allow the sauce to thicken and reduce.

Add the capers, dried oregano and tarragon, then turn off the heat and leave the mixture to cool.

For the pastry, rub the flour and butter together in a mixing bowl until they form a crumbly texture. Add the cold water a little at a time until you form a soft ball of dough.

Transfer the pastry to a clean worktop and knead for 30 seconds, then leave the pastry to rest for 10 minutes.

Once rested, roll the pastry out to 1cm thick and line a 24cm pie tin with the pastry before spooning the chicken mixture on top.

In a separate bowl, mix the breadcrumbs and parmesan together with a tablespoon of olive oil and scatter it over the top of the chicken pie filling.

Trim the edges of the pastry then bake in a preheated oven at 170°c for 30 to 40 minutes, or until the top becomes golden in colour and the pastry is crisp.

TUSCAN BREAD SOUP

Prep time: 10 minutes | Cooking time: 20 minutes | Serves 4

This one brings back some memories. I discovered this recipe while I was in Tuscany visiting our friends Marina and Franchesco. It might seem a little strange to put bread in your soup while it's cooking, but it makes the soup incredibly creamy, and it's the perfect way to use up leftover bread.

INGREDIENTS:

175g ciabatta bread, cut into chunks
1 onion, chopped
2 tbsp olive oil
3 cloves of garlic, chopped
Pinch of dried chilli flakes
Pinch of salt and pepper
400g ripe tomatoes
1 x 400g tin of chopped tomatoes
400ml water
1 vegetable stock cube
Fresh basil leaves, to serve
Extra-virgin olive oil, to serve

HERE'S HOW:

To make the croutons, place the ciabatta chunks onto an oven tray and bake for 15 minutes at 160°c until crisp and dry. Set them aside until later.

Place the chopped onions into a pan with the olive oil, garlic, and chilli flakes. Season with a little salt and pepper and cook for 5 minutes.

Add the fresh and tinned tomatoes, then swill the empty tin with the water and add to the pan.

Pop in the stock cube, then bring to the boil before turning down to simmer for 10 to 15 minutes or until the onions have softened.

Add three quarters of the bread, stir, then remove from the heat and use a stick blender to blend until smooth. Taste the soup and season if required.

Pour the soup into a bowl and top with the remaining croutons. Finish with fresh basil leaves and a drizzle of your best extra-virgin olive oil.

Scan the QR Code to watch how to make this recipe

WILD MUSHROOM AND RIGATONI BAKE

Prep time: 20 minutes | Cooking time: 30 minutes | Serves 4

I hated mushrooms as a kid, but once I was taught how to cook them properly, I realised just how delicious they could be. If you spend time cooking the mushrooms, seasoning them well, and making sure all the water evaporates out of them, they are truly delicious. This pasta bake is the perfect way to serve them: rich, creamy and crunchy on the top.

INGREDIENTS:

360g rigatoni pasta

200g wild mushrooms

1 tsp salt

1 clove of garlic, chopped

1 tsp fresh rosemary, chopped

1 tsp fresh thyme, chopped

30g salted butter

100ml dry white wine

70ml double cream

½ lemon, juiced

100g breadcrumbs

2 tbsp olive oil

60g parmesan, grated

HERE'S HOW:

Preheat the oven to 180°c.

Cook the pasta in a large pan of salted boiling water for 8 minutes. (Once the pasta is al dente, drain it and set it aside, but make sure to reserve some pasta cooking water for the sauce.)

Meanwhile, tear the mushrooms into pieces, but not too small as you want to keep their texture.

Add the mushrooms to a large, heated frying pan with a drizzle of olive oil and a good seasoning of salt. (The salt will draw out the moisture from the mushrooms so it can evaporate during the cooking process - that's the secret to a well-cooked mushroom.)

Add the chopped garlic and gently fry. Once all the liquid from the mushrooms has evaporated, scatter in the chopped herbs and butter. Pour in the white wine and bring to the boil to reduce the liquid.

Take 50ml, or one ladle, of pasta cooking water from the saucepan and add it to the mushrooms.

Swirl the pan to bring the sauce together, then pour in the cream and stir. Add the lemon juice to balance out the richness, season to taste, then stir in the al dente pasta.

For the topping, mix the breadcrumbs with 2 tablespoons of olive oil and 20g of grated parmesan cheese.

Use your hand to squeeze the breadcrumbs, as this will help the oil soak into the bread and make the crumbs taste amazing.

Transfer the pasta and mushroom sauce into an ovenproof dish and top with the breadcrumbs and remaining parmesan. Finish with a drizzle of olive oil and bake for 15 minutes or until golden brown.

 Scan the QR Code to watch how to make this recipe

CRISPY ASIAN-STYLE CHICKEN TENDERS

Prep time: 15 minutes | Cooking time: 20 minutes | Serves 4

This recipe is for my son, Thomas, who loves his crispy chicken. I created this dish when I found a leftover jar of cranberry sauce at Christmastime and thought to myself, "What can I make with this?" I'm sure most households end up with leftover cranberry sauce in the back of the fridge, so get yours out and make this recipe – it's delicious!

INGREDIENTS:

FOR THE CHICKEN

2 boneless and skinless chicken breasts (180g each)

1 tsp onion powder

1 tsp salt

100g plain flour

2 large free-range eggs

100g panko breadcrumbs

2 tbsp white sesame seeds

2 tbsp black sesame seeds

FOR THE DIPPING SAUCE

1 jar cranberry sauce

3 tbsp light soy sauce

1 lime, juiced

1 tsp Korean gochujang chilli paste

TO SERVE

3 spring onions

1 handful of fresh coriander

HERE'S HOW:

Preheat the oven to 170°c.

Cut the chicken breast into 1cm-thick slices and place in a bowl with the dried onion powder, salt, and flour. Mix to fully coat the chicken.

Crack the eggs into a separate bowl and whisk with a fork. Add the breadcrumbs to another bowl and stir in the white and black sesame seeds.

Dip the floured chicken into the beaten egg, then coat in the sesame breadcrumbs.

Make sure the chicken is completely coated before placing it on a plate. Don't lay them on top of each other - you want the breadcrumbs to stay dry so they'll crisp up when fried.

Preheat a shallow nonstick frying pan with 3 to 4 tablespoons of olive oil. When the oil is hot, carefully lay the chicken in the pan and cook for 3 to 4 minutes on each side or until golden and crispy.

Remove the chicken from the pan and transfer onto a baking tray. Cook the chicken in the oven for a further 10 minutes to ensure it is cooked through.

While the chicken is cooking, place the cranberry sauce into a saucepan with the soy sauce, lime juice, and the Korean chilli paste. Gently heat the sauce, while stirring, to bring the flavours together.

Serve the crispy chicken with chopped spring onion, freshly chopped coriander, and the spicy cranberry sauce.

Weekend Feasts

WEEKEND FEASTS

This chapter is about enjoying food, good company and just spending time with the people that matter in your life. Cooking for others is something I love to do, and there's no better feeling than sharing your hard work and effort through food. Breaking bread with friends and family is the best way to spend a weekend, if you ask me.

CRUSHED POTATO BRAVAS WITH CHORIZO (ISH)

Prep time: 20 minutes | Cooking time: 40 minutes | Serves 4

This recipe is very much inspired by my good friend and colleague Carlos. Crushed potatoes roasted in the natural oils from the chorizo make culinary magic in the oven. This recipe is simple, easy to make, and wonderful to serve up and just tuck right into!

INGREDIENTS:

500g baby or new potatoes
1 tbsp salt
225g chorizo sausage
2 cloves of garlic
2 tbsp olive oil
1 tsp smoked paprika
Pinch of salt and pepper, to taste
1 tbsp sherry vinegar
1 handful of fresh coriander, chopped
Sour cream, to serve (optional)

HERE'S HOW:

Preheat the oven to 170°c.

Cook the potatoes in a large pan of salted boiling water until just tender, then drain and set aside.

Cut the chorizo sausage into 1cm slices and place into a large roasting tray. Add the garlic cloves, smashing them open to help release their flavour.

Place the potatoes onto the roasting tray and use a mug to squash them until they break open and flatten onto the tray.

Drizzle everything with a little olive oil and season with the smoked paprika and some salt and pepper, then mix so everything has an even coating.

Cook in the oven for 30 to 40 minutes or until the potatoes are crispy and crunchy.

Remove from the oven and add the sherry vinegar before stirring together. Finish with a sprinkle of chopped coriander and serve with sour cream.

 Scan the QR Code to watch how to make this recipe

FENNEL AND PECORINO RISOTTO

Prep time: 15 minutes | Cooking time: 20 minutes | Serves 4

This recipe was inspired by a trip to Milan - the home of risotto! It may not be a traditional Italian recipe, but I think it works really well. When I made this dish for a set of chefs, it got their seal of approval, so that's good enough for me!

INGREDIENTS:

1.5L vegetable stock

2 tbsp olive oil

2 fennel bulbs, finely chopped

2 cloves of garlic, chopped

400g risotto rice

250ml white wine

50g pecorino or parmesan (or vegetarian alternative), half finely grated, half shaved

50g butter

Pinch of salt and pepper, to taste

2 handfuls of soft herbs (such as basil, chervil or chives)

1 lemon, halved

HERE'S HOW:

Warm the vegetable stock and leave it on a low heat (this'll help to keep the flow of the cooking process).

Place a large, nonstick, shallow pan onto the heat with a splash of olive oil. Scatter the fennel and garlic into the pan with a sprinkle of salt, then cook for 4 to 5 minutes to draw out the moisture and get the flavours going.

Add the rice and cook for a further 5 minutes to allow the rice to crack. This will help release the starch from the rice and result in a creamy risotto without adding cream.

Pour in the white wine and boil away the alcohol, then pour in the warm stock a little at a time while stirring at the same time, making sure the stock has been absorbed before adding more. Risotto is a labour of love, so it's important to stay with the pan and keep stirring and adding the stock until the rice is tender, but not too soft.

When tender, add in the grated cheese and butter, then stir together. Taste for seasoning and add salt and pepper if required.

To finish, stir in the chopped herbs and a squeeze of lemon juice before plating up. (I like to finish my risotto with more grated parmesan cheese and a drizzle of my best extra-virgin olive oil.)

NOTE:

If you fancy, you can add crispy Parma ham as a garnish. Just bake it in the oven for 10 minutes at 160°c until crisp and sprinkle on top.

 Scan the QR Code to watch how to make this recipe

FENNEL, MOZZARELLA AND CRISPY PARMA HAM

Prep time: 20 minutes | Cooking time: 10 minutes | Serves 4

This simple, Italian-inspired salad is based around a classic combination of ingredients. Crisp fennel, creamy mozzarella and salty Parma ham just work together! This one's perfect for serving in the middle of the table with dinner.

INGREDIENTS:

4 slices of Parma ham (or any dry-cured ham of choice)
2 fennel bulbs
½ lemon, juiced
1 red chilli
1 tsp fennel seeds
1 tbsp white wine vinegar
3 tbsp extra-virgin olive oil
Pinch of salt and pepper, to taste
2 balls of buffalo mozzarella
1 handful of fresh basil

HERE'S HOW:

Place the slices of ham onto a sheet of parchment paper and cook in a preheated oven at 160°c for about 10 minutes until crisp. When the ham is ready, remove it from the oven and leave to cool.

Meanwhile, cut the fennel bulbs in half lengthways and carefully remove the core from the base of the vegetable. Slice the fennel as thinly as possible and place in a mixing bowl with the lemon juice. Give it a mix to help the juice take the raw edge off the fennel.

To make the dressing, cut the red chilli lengthways down the middle and remove the seeds. Slice into matchsticks, then gather and chop into small pieces.

Add the chilli to a mixing bowl with the fennel seeds, vinegar and extra-virgin olive oil. Season the dressing with a little salt and pepper before whisking together. Taste for seasoning, then set aside.

Slice the mozzarella into 1cm-thick slices, then arrange it on a large plate - without overlapping - before spooning over a little of the dressing. Season with salt and pepper before placing the sliced fennel on top.

Drizzle over the remaining dressing, then scatter the basil over the top. Finish with the crispy ham by crumbling it over the top of the salad before serving.

MISO GLAZED SALMON WITH PICKLED WATERMELON SALSA

Prep time: 15 minutes, plus 1 hour marinating | Cooking time: 25 minutes | Serves 4

This recipe is so easy to make, but let me tell you, it is absolutely packed with flavour! The combination of savoury miso and soy, sweet brown sugar, and a tang of vinegar works perfectly on top of the salmon. Serve with pickled watermelon salsa to cut through the oily fish.

INGREDIENTS:

FOR THE SALMON

2 tbsp miso paste

2 tbsp light soft brown sugar

2 tbsp white vinegar

2 tbsp soy sauce

600g fillet fresh salmon

FOR THE SALSA

200g watermelon

100ml white wine vinegar

2 shallots, finely chopped

3 tbsp olive oil

2 tbsp coriander leaf

HERE'S HOW:

Combine the miso, sugar, vinegar and soy in a bowl. Then, place the salmon portion onto a nonstick baking tray and cover with the miso paste mixture. Leave to marinate for 1 hour in the fridge.

Meanwhile, cut the watermelon into small cubes and coat with white wine vinegar. Leave to pickle for 30 minutes before adding the chopped shallots, olive oil and coriander leaf.

Cook the marinated salmon in a preheated oven at 170°c for 20 to 25 minutes. When cooked, remove from the oven and serve with a generous scoop of the watermelon salsa.

 Scan the QR Code to watch how to make this recipe

SAVOURY BAKLAVA

Prep time: 20 minutes | Cooking time: 40 minutes | Serves 4

This recipe isn't very traditional, but it's inspired by a Greek and Turkish dessert called baklava. Layers of amazing flavour combinations is the goal with this dish. I created it in 2024 while working with California Prunes and it's possibly one of my favourite recipes, so I felt I had to share it with you. My top tip would be to drizzle the honey on top of the baklava once it's baked as it makes all the difference.

INGREDIENTS:

1 bunch of spring onions, chopped
200g mixed nuts
4 tbsp pumpkin seeds
150g California prunes, chopped
225g halloumi
200g feta
1 lemon
270g filo pastry
80g butter, melted
2 tbsp sesame seeds
½ tsp dried chilli flakes
2 tbsp honey

HERE'S HOW:

Preheat the oven to 180°c.

Add the spring onions to a bowl with the nuts, seeds, and chopped California Prunes.

Grate the halloumi cheese straight into the bowl and crumble in the feta.

Cut the lemon in half and squeeze the juice into the bowl before stirring together.

Trim the filo pastry sheets to fit an ovenproof dish, then brush the bottom of the tin with melted butter. Place one sheet of the filo into the bottom of the tin, brush with more melted butter, then top with another sheet. Repeat this process with another sheet to make up three layers in total.

Top with one third of the cheese, nut and prune mixture, then repeat the process twice more with the layers of buttered filo pastry and filling to give you three layers of filling.

Finish with a final three layers of the filo pastry and brush with the remaining melted butter.

Using a sharp knife, cut a diamond pattern into the pie, making sure you cut all the way through to the base.

Scatter with sesame seeds and chilli flakes before baking in the oven for 40 minutes or until golden and crisp. Once baked, drizzle with honey before serving.

Scan the QR Code to watch how to make this recipe

SKIRT BEEF AND CHIMICHURRI

Prep time: 15 minutes | Cooking time: 12 minutes | Serves 4

Skirt beef is an amazing cut of beef, and more people should be using it. It's the perfect steak to cook as a whole piece. Once your steak is ready, just carve it up and serve it up with this amazing Argentinian salsa… chimichurri!

INGREDIENTS:

FOR THE BEEF

1kg skirt beef (ideally from your local butcher)
2 tbsp olive oil
2 tbsp sea salt
2 tbsp fresh black pepper
40g salted butter

FOR THE CHIMICHURRI

60g flat leaf parsley, chopped
1 red onion, finely chopped
1 clove of garlic
1 red chilli, finely chopped
60ml red wine vinegar
150ml extra-virgin olive oil
Pinch of salt and pepper, to taste

HERE'S HOW:

Using a sharp knife, trim any excess fat and sinew from the skirt beef as it doesn't always render during the cooking process. Pat the meat dry with a piece of kitchen paper, then drizzle with olive oil.

Rub the oil all over the meat before seasoning well with salt and plenty of black pepper.

Preheat a large frying pan, grill pan or cast-iron skillet. When the pan is really hot, place the beef in to cook. (Don't be tempted to move the meat around. Let the salt draw the moisture out and caramelise the beef. If you move it about, it won't sear.)

It's important to get a good strong sear around the outside of the beef. After approximately 5 to 6 minutes, turn it over, add the butter, and do the same on the other side.

While the steak cooks, prepare the chimichurri by combining all the ingredients in a small bowl.

Remove the steak from the pan and set aside to rest. If you rest the beef well, it'll be super tender and delicious, so don't underestimate the importance of this step! Let it relax before you carve across the grain of the meat, then serve with the chimichurri on top.

NOTE:

You can use a digital thermometer to check the core temperature of the beef: 50°c is rare, 55°c medium rare, 60°c medium, 65°c medium well, and 70°c well done.

 Scan the QR Code to watch how to make this recipe

HONEYCOMB WITH CHOCOLATE AND SEA SALT

Prep time: 1 hour 30 minutes | Cooking time:20 minutes | Serves 4

Once you've made homemade honeycomb, you won't go back to the shop-bought stuff. By adding a hint of sea salt and a drizzle of good quality dark chocolate, you won't be able to stop nibbling this deliciously sweet treat!

INGREDIENTS:

200g caster sugar
5 tbsp golden syrup
2 tsp bicarbonate of soda
100g dark chocolate (70% cocoa)
1 tbsp sea salt flakes

HERE'S HOW:

Line a 20cm square brownie tin with a sheet of parchment paper or silicone.

Stir the caster sugar and golden syrup together in a deep saucepan over a gentle heat until the sugar has melted. Make sure to keep it on a low heat, and don't let the mixture bubble until the sugar grains have fully dissolved.

Once melted, simmer until you achieve a golden, amber-coloured caramel, then - as quickly as you can - turn off the heat, add in the bicarbonate of soda, and stir with a wooden spoon until it has all disappeared and the mixture is bubbling. Immediately transfer to the brownie tin – be careful, it will be very hot! The mixture will continue bubbling in the tin.

Simply leave it for 1 hour to 1 hour and 30 minutes to cool and harden. Melt the chocolate while it cools.

Once the honeycomb has completely cooled and set, use the paper to lift it out of the tin, then drop it on the kitchen worktop so that it breaks up into random chunks.

Drizzle the melted dark chocolate over the honeycomb and finish with a sprinkle of sea salt while the chocolate is still runny. Leave to set, then store in an airtight container for up to 2 weeks.

WHITE ONION SOUP WITH SODA BREAD

Prep time: 30 minutes, plus 30 minutes cooling | Cooking time: 1 hour 25 minutes | Serves 4-6

This soup is really easy and relies on just two basic ingredients, but it proves that great things can happen when you know how to get the best out of simple ingredients! This soup becomes sweet and creamy just by baking the onions whole in their skins. Try serving it with my quick and easy soda bread – they go perfect together.

INGREDIENTS:

FOR THE ONION SOUP
3 large white onions, unpeeled

1 garlic bulb

2 tbsp olive oil

Pinch of salt and pepper, to taste

500ml vegetable stock

50ml double cream (optional, if you like it creamy)

FOR THE BREAD
500g self-raising flour

1 tsp bicarbonate of soda

1 tbsp nigella seeds

1 tsp salt

1 tbsp plain yoghurt

1 tsp honey

300ml water

HERE'S HOW:

FOR THE SOUP
Preheat the oven to 160°c.

Put the onions and garlic in a large roasting tray, drizzle with olive oil, and season with salt and pepper. Place in the preheated oven and cook for an hour or until soft.

Remove from the oven and leave to cool for 30 minutes. Use a pair of sharp scissors to cut the root off the onion, then squeeze the onions and garlic out of their skins and into a blender. Add the hot vegetable stock and blend until smooth. Finally, add the cream (if using) and season to taste.

Place the onion skins in the bin, but keep all the roasting juices from the tray to drizzle over the soup (I call this "the Marmite", because this is where the big flavour is!). Serve the soup with thick slices of soda bread.

FOR THE SODA BREAD
Preheat the oven to 170°c.

Place the flour, bicarbonate of soda, nigella seeds and salt into a mixing bowl, and blend together with your hand.

Make a well in the centre of the flour mix, then pour in the yoghurt, honey and three quarters of the water. Use one hand in a claw shape to roll it around the bowl until it forms a soft ball of dough. Add the remaining water if needed.

Transfer the dough onto a lightly floured work surface and shape it into a loaf (don't knead this bread or it will become tough and dense).

Place the dough into a nonstick loaf tin, score the top with a bread knife, then bake for 20 to 25 minutes.

LAMB WITH NECTARINE, PISTACHIO AND FETA

Prep time: 15 minutes, plus 1 hour marinating | Cooking time: 10 minutes | Serves 4

Lamb and nectarines might not be the first flavour combination you think of, but let me tell you these two ingredients work so well together. Serve them on top of my delicious pistachio and feta dip with pitta breads and then you're really talking!

INGREDIENTS:

FOR THE LAMB KEBABS

1 tbsp cumin seeds

1 tbsp coriander seeds

2 cloves of garlic

1 tbsp sesame seeds

1 lemon, zested

1 tbsp salt

1 tsp black pepper

2 tbsp olive oil

1 tbsp fresh rosemary, chopped

750g British lamb leg or rump, cut into 3cm cubes

4 nectarines

FOR THE PISTACHIO AND FETA DIP

100g pistachios

100g feta

100g extra-virgin olive oil

3 cloves of garlic

1 handful of coriander

1 handful of fresh mint

½ lemon, juiced

Pinch of salt and pepper, to taste

TO SERVE

200g salad leaves

8 pitta breads

HERE'S HOW:

FOR THE LAMB KEBABS

To make the lamb marinade, add the cumin and coriander seeds to a dry frying pan and toast on a medium heat for 3 to 4 minutes. When the spices are toasted and your kitchen is full of their fragrant aroma, pour them into a pestle and mortar and grind to a powder.

Add the spices to a mixing bowl with the garlic, sesame seeds, lemon zest, salt, pepper, olive oil and chopped rosemary. Stir the mixture together.

Place the lamb into a large mixing bowl with the marinade and stir to coat, then put it in the fridge for 1 hour to marinate.

When ready to cook, cut the nectarines into wedges and thread onto a wooden kebab stick, alternating with the diced marinated lamb.

Cook the lamb on the barbecue or grill it for 8 to 10 minutes until cooked through.

FOR THE PISTACHIO AND FETA DIP

Place all the ingredients into a food processor, blend until smooth, and season to taste.

When the lamb is cooked, serve with warm pitta bread, salad leaves, and the dip.

 Scan the QR Code to watch how to make this recipe

TIKKA SALMON AND SPINACH PIE

Prep time: 20 minutes, plus 20 minutes marinating | Cooking time: 40 minutes | Serves 4-6

A fish pie with a twist. I love this recipe as it's packed with flavour, easy to prepare and delicious to eat. It's a lot lighter than a typical fish pie, so it can be enjoyed any time of the year.

INGREDIENTS:

450g frozen spinach
1 red onion, finely chopped
1 thumb ginger, finely grated
1 clove of garlic, finely grated
1 lemon, juiced and zested
2 large free-range eggs
Pinch of salt and pepper, to taste
4 tbsp Greek-style yoghurt
2 tbsp Indian Spice Mix (see page 176)
600g fresh salmon
50g margarine or butter, melted
3 tbsp nigella seeds
270g filo pastry (approx. 7 sheets)

HERE'S HOW:

Preheat the oven to 165°c.

Remove the spinach from the freezer and place in a colander over a bowl to thaw. When thawed, transfer to a clean tea towel, then draw the corners together and squeeze out all the excess water.

Place the red onion in a mixing bowl with the grated ginger, garlic and lemon zest, then add the spinach along with the eggs. Season with salt and pepper before stirring together.

In a separate bowl, combine the yoghurt, spice mix, lemon juice, and more salt and pepper to taste. Add the salmon, stir to coat, and leave to marinate for 20 minutes to develop the flavour.

Brush the melted butter on the bottom of a deep ovenproof dish that measures approximately 30cm by 20cm. Sprinkle some of the nigella seeds and a little more of the Indian Spice Mix on top, then layer the pastry into the tin. Make sure each sheet overlaps and hangs over the sides of the tin, so when you fold the pastry on top, it will cover the filling.

Once all seven sheets of pastry are in, brush with more melted butter and spread the spinach mixture on the base. Lay the salmon on top of the spinach, then fold all the excess pastry into the middle. Brush the top with the remaining butter and scatter over the rest of the nigella seeds.

Bake the pie for 30 to 40 minutes until golden and crispy on the top.

 Scan the QR Code to watch how to make this recipe

BALSAMIC GLAZED CHICKEN POT ROAST

Prep time: 20 minutes | Cooking time: 1 hour 40 minutes | Serves 4-6

This recipe is definitely a perfect weekend feast. It's ideal for putting on to cook on a Sunday morning before you head out for a walk. When you return, you'll have a pot full of the most delicious food that you can pop down in the middle of the table and enjoy. What's even better is that it all cooks in one pan.

INGREDIENTS:

100ml balsamic vinegar
50g light soft brown sugar
300g chicken stock
1 garlic bulb, cut in half
90g sun-dried tomatoes
Large whole chicken
1 fennel bulb
2 white onions
1kg Maris Piper potatoes
2 bay leaves

HERE'S HOW:

Preheat the oven to 180°c.

Place the vinegar, sugar, chicken stock, garlic, and sun-dried tomatoes into a large saucepan. Add the whole chicken, breast side down, so it's immersed in the liquid.

Cut the fennel into thirds, the onions into sixths, and the potatoes in half, and add them to the pan along with the bay leaves. Season with salt, pepper and a drizzle of olive oil, then roast for 1 hour with the lid on to trap the heat.

After 1 hour, remove from the oven, take the lid off, and carefully turn the chicken over so it is breast side up before returning to the oven for 30 to 40 minutes.

When everything is cooked, remove the chicken and vegetables from the oven and transfer to a serving platter.

Place the pan and its juices onto a hob and boil until it reduces by half, then serve this amazing sauce alongside your pot roast.

 Scan the QR Code to watch how to make this recipe

WHIPPED FETA DIP WITH HONEY AND GARLIC

Prep time: 10 minutes | Cooking time: 25 minutes | Serves 4-6

Whipped feta is creamy and rich in flavour, and this one's served up with my unique garlic-flavoured honey for the perfect taste combo. This goes great with a barbecue and lots of flatbreads. Any leftovers are perfect for stirring through pasta the next day, but if I'm honest, we never have any left – it's too yummy!

INGREDIENTS:

300ml jar of clear honey

20 cloves of garlic, peeled

1 tbsp fresh thyme

1 red chilli, sliced lengthways (optional)

200g feta

100g ricotta

Fresh black pepper, to taste

2 tbsp black and white sesame seeds

HERE'S HOW:

Place the honey, garlic, thyme and chilli (if desired) into a small saucepan on a medium heat. Simmer for about 25 minutes until the garlic is soft and squidgy.

When the garlic is ready, carefully remove from the heat and leave to cool for 10 minutes before transferring to a preserving jar. This'll keep in the fridge for 4 to 6 weeks, no problem.

Whisk the feta and ricotta in a bowl until smooth and season with fresh black pepper. Keep in the fridge until ready to serve.

To serve, spoon the mixture onto a plate and spread it to the edges with the back of a spoon, then top with some of the honey and garlic and a sprinkling of sesame seeds. Enjoy with delicious, warm flatbreads.

DESPERATE DAN COW PIE

Prep time: 55 minutes, plus 30 mins resting | Cooking time: 3 hours and 35 minutes | Serves 6-8

This pie is rich, beefy, and all wrapped up in the perfect crispy pastry. This recipe should be the benchmark for all pies in your kitchen. I can't stress how important it is to buy the right cut of beef for this recipe. Beef shin is the minimum, but cheek is best if you can get it.

INGREDIENTS:

FOR THE FILLING
2 tbsp vegetable oil
900g stewing beef, cut into bite-sized cubes (I prefer to use beef shin)
Pinch of salt and pepper, to taste
2 large onions, finely chopped
3 cloves of garlic, minced
2 tbsp plain flour
2 carrots, peeled and diced
2 celery sticks, diced
500ml beef broth or stock
300ml Malbec wine (I use Beefsteak Club)
2 bay leaves
2 sprigs of thyme

FOR THE PASTRY
150g cold butter, cubed
300g plain flour
3-4 tbsp ice-cold water
1 large free-range egg, beaten (for egg wash)

HERE'S HOW:

FOR THE FILLING
Heat the vegetable oil in a large, heavy-bottomed pan over medium to high heat. Season the beef with salt and pepper and sear it in the hot pan until browned on all sides. Remove and set aside.

Add the chopped onions and garlic to the same pan and sauté until the onion becomes translucent. Sprinkle the flour over the onions and garlic and stir to make a roux. Cook for a few minutes to eliminate the raw flour taste.

Return the seared beef to the pan, then add the carrots and celery. Pour in the beef broth and red wine, then stir well to combine. Add the bay leaves and thyme sprigs, then reduce the heat to low, cover, and simmer for 2 to 3 hours, or until the beef is tender and the sauce has thickened. Remove the bay leaves and thyme sprigs when done.

FOR THE PASTRY
While the filling is simmering, prepare the pastry. Combine the cold cubed butter and flour in a food processor and pulse until the mixture resembles coarse breadcrumbs. Add the ice-cold water gradually and pulse until the dough comes together, but be careful not to over-mix.

Divide the pastry dough into two portions with one slightly larger than the other. Wrap each part in cling film and refrigerate for at least 30 minutes.

TO ASSEMBLE THE PIE
Preheat the oven to 190°c.

Roll out the larger portion of pastry on a floured surface so it's big enough to line the bottom and sides of a greased 9-inch (23cm) pie dish. Pour the beef filling into the pastry-lined dish.

Roll out the smaller portion of pastry to create a lid for the pie, then place the pastry lid over the filling. Seal the edges by crimping with a fork, then cut a few small slits in the top to allow steam to escape.

Brush the top of the pie with the beaten egg to give it a beautiful golden finish, then bake in the oven for 30 to 35 minutes, or until the pastry is golden brown and the filling is bubbling.

Allow the Desperate Dan Cow Pie to cool slightly before serving. It's perfect served with mashed potatoes and your favourite green vegetables.

NOTE: You can double the filling and freeze it for another day. That way, you only need to make the pastry, or you can simply serve it up as a stew.

 Scan the QR Code to watch how to make this recipe

GREEK LAMB MEATBALL BAKE

Prep time: 15 minutes | Cooking time: 40 minutes | Serves 4

This recipe takes everything I know and love about Greek food and combines it into one convenient traybake. Make sure the tomatoes are a similar size to your meatballs so they burst when they cook and make the most delicious tomato sauce. It will take you back to your last visit to a sun-drenched Greek island.

INGREDIENTS:

500g minced lamb

2 cloves of garlic, chopped or crushed

1 tsp dried oregano

1 tbsp dried mint

2 tbsp breadcrumbs

3 red onions, cut into sixths

2 lemons, quartered

600g cherry tomatoes (don't use huge tomatoes as they won't cook)

4 tbsp extra-virgin olive oil

100g Kalamata olives

1 handful of flat leaf parsley, chopped

75g feta

4 pitta breads

HERE'S HOW:

Place the minced lamb into a bowl with the garlic, oregano, mint and breadcrumbs. Season with a little salt and pepper then mix with your hands.

Roll out the meatballs using wet hands. This'll help to form nice, smooth meatballs and prevent the meat from sticking to your hand. This recipe makes 12 meatballs, about 50g each.

Place the meatballs onto a deep, nonstick baking tray or dish, then add the onions, lemons, and whole cherry tomatoes. Drizzle with extra-virgin olive oil, sprinkle with a little salt and pepper, then add the olives and cook in the oven for 40 minutes.

Finish off with parsley and a crumbling of feta, then serve with pitta bread.

Scan the QR Code to watch how to make this recipe

PROPER PARKIN

Prep time: 25 minutes | Cooking time: 45 minutes | Serves 9

My mother-in-law, Brenda, makes proper parkin, as she was born and bred in Yorkshire. This recipe is a nod to all the lovely parkins we've had over the years, and I wanted to share this family recipe.

INGREDIENTS:

FOR THE PARKIN

200g unsalted butter

135g treacle

150g golden syrup

85g dark soft brown sugar

250g self-raising flour

100g pinhead or coarse oatmeal

1 tsp ground ginger

1 large free-range egg

4 tbsp milk

FOR THE GLAZE

200ml ginger beer

HERE'S HOW:

Preheat the oven to 160°c and line a 20cm square brownie tin with parchment paper.

Place the butter, treacle, syrup, and sugar in a shallow pan and melt together.

Meanwhile combine the flour, oatmeal, and ginger in a bowl.

Once the syrups, sugar and butter have melted, remove from the heat, and pour into the centre of the bowl with the flour and oatmeal. Quickly add the egg and milk before stirring together.

Transfer the mixture to the brownie tin and bake for 45 minutes or until the top of the cake is firm to the touch.

For the glaze, boil the ginger beer in a saucepan until it becomes syrupy, then brush it over the top of the cake while it's still warm.

VEGAN MEATLOAF WITH BLUEBERRY AND CARAMELISED ONION CHUTNEY

Prep time: 40 minutes | Cooking time: 45 minutes | Serves 4-6

Topped with luscious blueberries and caramelised onions, this vegan meatloaf is absolutely mouthwatering. This recipe combines the hearty flavours of a classic meatloaf with a sweet and tangy chutney made from fresh blueberries and slowly caramelised onions. It is a delightful blend of savoury and sweet, perfect for impressing guests.

INGREDIENTS:

3 tbsp olive oil

2 white onions, finely diced

3 carrots, peeled and finely diced

3 celery sticks, finely diced

5 cloves of garlic, minced

2 x 400g tins of chickpeas, drained

20g fresh breadcrumbs

3 tbsp ground flaxseed

5 tbsp nutritional yeast

3 tbsp dark soy sauce

3 tbsp vegan Worcestershire sauce (I use Henderson's Relish)

2 tbsp brown sauce

1 tsp liquid smoke (I use Stubbs)

200g frozen blueberries

2 red onions, finely diced

HERE'S HOW:

Preheat the oven to 190°c and grease and line a loaf tin.

Warm the oil over a medium heat then add the white onions, carrots, celery, and garlic. Sauté until translucent and set aside.

Meanwhile, mash the chickpeas in a large saucepan and bring to a medium heat. Add the sautéed vegetables, breadcrumbs, ground flaxseed, nutritional yeast, soy sauce, vegan Worcestershire sauce, brown sauce, and liquid smoke. Cook for 10 minutes.

Meanwhile, tip the blueberries into the base of the loaf tin and scatter the chopped red onion on top. Press in the vegan meatloaf mixture, taking care not to displace the berries and chopped onion, before baking for 45 minutes.

Allow to rest for 5 minutes before turning it out onto a cutting board, slicing, and serving.

BUTTERNUT SQUASH SOUP

Prep time: 20 minutes | Cooking time: 30 minutes | Serves 4

Butternut squash is one of my favourite vegetables to turn into a delicious, rich and velvety soup! Serving it up with a bunch of spices and fresh herbs makes every mouthful delicious. This soup is the perfect winter warmer.

INGREDIENTS:

2 white onions, chopped
1 large butternut squash, peeled and cubed
2 tbsp olive oil
1 tsp salt
2 tbsp harissa paste (1 for the soup; 1 for the dressing)
1L vegetable stock
1 lemon, juiced
1 tsp sesame seeds
1 tbsp coriander, chopped
1 tbsp mint, chopped
Pinch of salt and pepper, to taste

HERE'S HOW:

Place the onion, squash and olive oil into a large, deep saucepan. Turn to a medium heat and season with salt to draw out the moisture and bring out the flavour.

After about 10 minutes of cooking, add 1 tablespoon of harissa and the stock, then bring to the boil before turning down to a simmer for 20 minutes.

When the squash is soft and tender, blend until smooth in a liquidiser or using a stick blender.

Mix the remaining harissa, lemon juice, sesame seeds and a little extra olive oil in a small bowl to make a delicious dressing. (The harissa and lemon will cut through the rich, velvety texture of the soup.)

Finish the soup with a drizzle of the dressing and fresh herbs for a knockout winter-warming soup.

Season to taste with a little salt and pepper before serving.

FENNEL SAUSAGE WELLINGTON

Prep time: 45 minutes | Cooking time: 30 minutes | Serves 4-6

I have a reputation for baking some seriously good sausage rolls, so I thought it was time to take that tasty handheld snack and make it the star of the show. Pork and fennel make a great flavour combination and work so well in this buttery pastry parcel.

INGREDIENTS:

225g sausages, skins removed

1 fennel bulb, finely chopped

1 cooking apple, peeled and grated

4 fresh sage leaves

1 handful of flat leaf parsley, chopped

2 tsp wholegrain mustard

50g breadcrumbs

2 large free-range eggs (1 for the filling; 1 for an egg wash)

500g puff pastry

1 tsp fennel seeds

HERE'S HOW:

Preheat the oven to 170°c.

Place the sausages in a mixing bowl with the fennel and apple. Roll up the sage leaves and chop before adding to the bowl along with the chopped parsley, mustard, breadcrumbs and an egg.

Mix with a clean hand to make sure all the ingredients are well combined, then set the sausage filling to one side for 20 minutes. This allows the breadcrumbs to absorb the moisture while you roll out the pastry.

Cut the pastry in half and dust with flour before rolling out into 2 rectangles, approximately 50cm long by 15cm wide. Crack the other egg into a small bowl and beat well.

Place the sausage filling down the middle of the pastry, then brush the edges with beaten egg.

Roll out the remaining pastry to the same size as the base, then cut the pastry using a lattice cutter and lay it on top of the sausage meat.

Trim the edges and transfer to a lined baking tray. Brush with more beaten egg, sprinkle with fennel seeds, and bake in the oven for 30 minutes or until the pastry is golden and crisp.

 Scan the QR Code to watch how to make this recipe

PICKLED GARLIC CRISPY CHICKEN

Prep time: 35 minutes | Cooking time: 15 minutes | Serves 4

I love a chicken kiev but, more often than not, you go to all that effort to lock in the garlic butter only to have it run out and burn onto the tray during the cooking process. So, for this recipe, I've decided to take the butter out (of the chicken, that is!). This recipe doesn't use just any garlic butter: it's pickled garlic butter. The acidity of the pickled garlic cuts through the rich butter perfectly. It's so delicious, it's dangerous. You've been warned!

INGREDIENTS:

100ml white wine vinegar
4 cloves of garlic, peeled
4 chicken breasts
80g plain flour
3 large free-range eggs, beaten
180g panko breadcrumbs
2 tbsp olive oil
70g butter
1 tbsp rosemary
1 tbsp thyme
1 bay leaf

HERE'S HOW:

Preheat the oven to 170°c.

To make the pickled garlic, heat the vinegar in a shallow pan and add the peeled garlic cloves.

Simmer the vinegar for 2 to 3 minutes, then remove from the heat and leave to cool. Store in a clean jam jar in the fridge, and it'll keep for up to 6 weeks.

Trim the chicken breasts then slice each of them horizontally to create four thin fillets.

Take three mixing bowls and put the flour in one, the beaten eggs in another and the panko breadcrumbs in a third. Dip the chicken into the flour, then into the beaten egg, and finally coat in the breadcrumbs. Place the breaded chicken onto a tray ready to cook.

Heat the olive oil in a large, nonstick frying pan, then cook the chicken fillets until golden and crisp on each side. Place the chicken back onto the baking tray and cook in the oven for a further 10 to 12 minutes or until cooked through.

Wipe the frying pan clean with a kitchen towel, then add the butter and herbs and allow the butter to melt and foam up a little. Slice the pickled garlic and stir into the foaming butter.

Return the cooked chicken to the pan of butter and serve.

NOTE:

I like to pickle four to five bulbs of garlic at once and keep them in a preserving jar. They're great for serving with all kinds of savoury dishes!

4-Ways With

4 WAYS WITH...

This is a style of cooking that opens up a world of opportunity around one dish. In this chapter, I wanted to share recipes that give you the freedom and flexibility in the kitchen to adjust, tweak and adapt to what's in your fridge and cupboards. It's important to have these kinds of recipes in your repertoire as it will give you the confidence to make small changes while cooking if you need too.

4 WAYS WITH VIETNAMESE DRESSING

This simple Vietnamese dressing is full of flavour and incredibly versatile. By adding lime, soy, mint and chilli together, you end up with a flavour profile that is sweet, sour, salty, spicy and umami. These elements combined are the essentials of Asian-style cookery.

VIETNAMESE DRESSING AND PICKLED ONIONS

Prep time: 10 minutes | Serves 4-6

INGREDIENTS:

FOR THE PICKLED ONIONS

2 red onions, finely sliced

2 limes, juiced

FOR THE VIETNAMESE DRESSING

100ml light soy sauce

4 limes, juiced

1 red chilli, chopped

30g fresh mint, chopped

HERE'S HOW:

For the pickled onion, place the onions in a bowl with the juice of both limes. Use your hands to mix and squeeze the onions to help speed up the pickle.

To make the dressing, place the soy sauce, lime juice and chopped chilli into a small mixing bowl. Stir to combine – it should be salty, yet tangy at the same time, with a nice balance of both flavours and a little heat from the chilli. Add the chopped fresh mint and set to one side, ready to serve alongside your dishes.

BELLY PORK

Prep time: 10 minutes, plus 20 minutes resting | Cooking time: 2 hour and 30 minutes | Serves 4

INGREDIENTS:

2kg belly pork, off the bone

2 tbsp olive oil

1 tbsp sea salt flakes

Vietnamese dressing and pickled onions, to serve

HERE'S HOW:

Preheat the oven to 180°c.

Using a sharp knife, cut small slices into the pork skin, approximately 0.5cm deep and 1cm apart.

Drizzle with 2 tablespoons of olive oil and season with plenty of sea salt flakes, then use your hands to rub the salt into the cuts.

Place the pork on a roasting tray with a grill rack or on a wire rack placed over an oven tray. Roast for 30 minutes before turning the heat down to 160°c and cooking for a further 2 hours until the pork skin is nice and crispy.

When the pork is cooked, remove it from the oven and let it rest for 20 minutes.

Carve into 2 to 3cm slices and serve topped with lots of the Vietnamese dressing and pickled red onions.

 Scan the QR Code to watch how to make this recipe

SPATCHCOCK CHICKEN

Prep time: 10 minutes, plus 10 minutes resting | Cooking time: 1 hour and 10 minutes | Serves 4

INGREDIENTS:

1 medium whole chicken

2 tbsp olive oil

Pinch of salt and pepper

Vietnamese dressing and pickled onions, to serve

HERE'S HOW:

Preheat the oven to 170°c.

To prepare the chicken, take a large, sharp knife and carefully cut down both sides of the backbone to remove it.

Turn the chicken over and flatten it out on a baking tray.

With the same knife, make three to four cuts down to the bone on the legs and thighs as well as a few cuts on the breast. These will help to speed up the cooking process.

Drizzle the bird with a little olive oil and season well with salt and pepper, then roast it for 1 hour and 10 minutes.

When the chicken is cooked, remove it from the oven and leave to rest for 10 minutes.

To serve, spoon over lots of the Vietnamese dressing and top with the pickled red onions.

SALMON FILLET

Prep time: 5 minutes | Cooking time: 20 minutes | Serves 4

INGREDIENTS:

600g salmon fillets

Drizzle of olive oil

Pinch of salt and pepper

Vietnamese dressing and pickled onions, to serve

HERE'S HOW:

Preheat the oven to 170°c.

Place the salmon onto a piece of parchment paper and season with olive oil, salt, and pepper before cooking in the oven for 15 to 20 minutes.

When the salmon is cooked, remove from the oven and spoon over lots of the Vietnamese dressing.

Serve with the pickled red onions for an amazing balance of flavour.

SESAME CRISPY AUBERGINE

Prep time: 15 minutes | Cooking time: 20 minutes | Serves 4

INGREDIENTS:

3 aubergines

1 tsp salt

70g plain flour

3 large free-range eggs, beaten

125g panko breadcrumbs

2 tbsp sesame seeds

Vietnamese dressing and pickled onions, to serve

HERE'S HOW:

Preheat the oven to 170°c.

Using a sharp knife, cut off the outer edges of the aubergine skin on either side as these are too tough to use. Then, cut each aubergine lengthways into 1cm-thick slices.

Place the slices of aubergine into a bowl and season with a little salt to draw out the moisture.

To coat the aubergine slices, place the flour into a shallow bowl, the beaten eggs into another bowl, and the breadcrumbs and sesame seeds into a third.

Flour the first slice of aubergine on both sides, then dip it into the beaten egg, making sure it's fully coated, then coat it in the breadcrumbs. Spend some time to make sure the breadcrumbs stick to the aubergine.

Repeat the process until you have coated all the slices, then place them on a baking tray.

Spray them with a little olive oil on both sides, then bake in the oven for 15 to 20 minutes or until golden and crispy.

Serve the crispy aubergine topped with the Vietnamese dressing and pickled red onions.

4 WAYS WITH BANANA BREAD

Don't let your sad old bananas go to waste – stick them in your freezer until you're ready to bake one of these fantastic banana bread recipes!

BLUEBERRY

Prep time: 15 minutes | Cooking time: 50 minutes | Makes 1 loaf (approx. 8 slices)

INGREDIENTS:

250g salted butter

250g caster sugar

4 large free-range eggs

1 lime, zested

1 tsp vanilla extract

2 ripe bananas, crushed with a fork until smooth

250g self-raising flour

100g blueberries (fresh or frozen)

HERE'S HOW:

Preheat the oven to 170°c.

Place the butter and sugar into a mixer and blend until light and fluffy.

Add the eggs, one at a time, and mix slowly until they're fully combined.

Stir in the lime zest, vanilla extract, and crushed bananas.

Sift in the flour and mix for 1 minute. (This might sound like a long time, but I like to slice and toast my banana bread for a weekend breakfast, and it helps if the cake is a little more robust. Extra mixing will develop the gluten a little and help turn it from a banana cake into a banana bread.)

Finally, gently stir in the blueberries so they don't break up in the mixture.

Pour the mix into a 2lb loaf tin and bake for 50 minutes until the top of the cake is firm to the touch.

Leave to cool before slicing, toasting and buttering (if you fancy it).

CINNAMON

Prep time: 15 minutes | Cooking time: 50 minutes | Makes 1 loaf (approx. 8 slices)

INGREDIENTS:

250g salted butter

250g light soft brown sugar

4 large free-range eggs

1 lemon, zested

1 tsp vanilla extract

2 ripe bananas, crushed with a fork until smooth

250g self-raising flour

1 tsp ground cinnamon

HERE'S HOW:

Preheat the oven to 170°c.

Place the butter and sugar into a mixer and blend until light and fluffy.

Add the eggs, one at a time, and mix slowly until they're fully combined.

Stir in the lemon zest, vanilla extract and crushed bananas.

Sift in the flour and cinnamon and mix for 1 minute. (This might sound like a long time, but I like to slice and toast my banana bread for a weekend breakfast, and it helps if the cake is a little more robust. Extra mixing will develop the gluten a little and help turn it from a banana cake into a banana bread.)

Pour the mix into a 2lb loaf tin and bake for 50 minutes until the top of the cake is firm to the touch.

Leave to cool before slicing, toasting and buttering (if you fancy it).

HALF-FAT CHOCOLATE BANANA BREAD

Prep time: 15 minutes | Cooking time: 50 minutes | Makes 1 loaf (approx. 8 slices)

INGREDIENTS:

125g margarine or butter

125g California prunes, chopped

200g golden caster sugar

4 large free-range eggs

2 ripe bananas, crushed with a fork until smooth

220g self-raising flour

30g cocoa powder

HERE'S HOW:

Preheat the oven to 170°c.

Blend the margarine and California prunes in a food processor to make the half-fat butter.

Place the half-fat butter and golden caster sugar into a mixer and blend until light and fluffy.

Add the eggs, one at a time, and mix slowly until they're fully combined, then stir in the crushed bananas.

Sift in the flour and cocoa powder and mix slowly until combined.

Pour the mix into a 2lb loaf tin and bake for 50 minutes until the top of the cake is firm to the touch.

Leave to cool before slicing.

GLUTEN-FREE BANANA BREAD WITH LEMON AND POPPY SEED

Prep time: 15 minutes | Cooking time: 50 minutes | Makes 1 loaf (approx. 8 slices)

INGREDIENTS:

250g salted butter

250g caster sugar

4 eggs

1 lemon, zested

1 tsp vanilla extract

2 ripe bananas, crushed with a fork until smooth

220g gluten-free self-raising flour

2 tbsp ground polenta

2 tbsp poppy seeds

HERE'S HOW:

Preheat the oven to 170°c.

Place the butter and sugar into a mixer and blend until light and fluffy.

Add the eggs, one at a time, and mix slowly until they're fully combined.

Stir in the lemon zest, vanilla extract and crushed bananas.

Sift in the flour, then add the ground polenta and poppy seeds and combine.

Pour the mix into a 2lb loaf tin and bake for 50 minutes until the top of the cake is firm to the touch.

Leave to cool before slicing.

4 WAYS WITH BURGERS

Everyone loves a good burger, whether you're a meat eater, vegetarian or fish lover. With these recipes, I've got it covered!

BHAJI BURGER

Prep time: 20 minutes, plus 20 minutes resting | Cooking time: 15 minutes | Serves 4

INGREDIENTS:

FOR THE CHUTNEY

6 tbsp mango chutney

1 grapefruit, peeled and cut into small segments

1 handful of fresh mint, chopped

FOR THE BURGERS

2 white onions sliced, thinly sliced

1 red onion, thinly sliced

½ tsp salt

1 tbsp cumin seeds

1 tsp turmeric

1 tsp curry powder

1 tbsp onion flakes

2 cloves of garlic, chopped finely

1 tsp fresh ginger, finely grated

1 sweet potato, grated

2 carrots, grated

250g halloumi, grated

4 tbsp gram flour

3 tbsp water

2 tbsp olive oil

TO SERVE

4 burger buns

Ribbons of cucumber

HERE'S HOW:

Mix the chutney ingredients together and set to one side.

To make the burgers, begin by placing the sliced onions and salt into a bowl. Squeeze the onions with one hand to help the salt penetrate the onions and soften them.

Add the spices, chopped garlic, and ginger, along with the grated sweet potato, carrot and halloumi. Mix until combined.

Scatter in the gram flour and pour over the water, then get your hands in and mix it all together.

Divide the mixture into four portions and, using wet hands, shape into burgers before placing them into the fridge to rest and firm up for 20 minutes.

Drizzle 2 tablespoons of oil into a large nonstick frying pan over a medium heat, then place the burgers into the pan. Cook for about 6 to 7 minutes on each side or until cooked through.

Serve the burgers in buns with the mango chutney mix and cucumber ribbons.

 Scan the QR Code to watch how to make this recipe

SALMON BURGER WITH TARRAGON BURGER SAUCE

Prep time: 10 minutes | Cooking time: 15 minutes | Serves 4

INGREDIENTS:

550g Alaskan sockeye salmon, skin removed and cut into chunks
1 clove of garlic
1 thumb of ginger, peeled and roughly chopped
2 tbsp flat leaf parsley, chopped
Pinch of salt and pepper

FOR THE SAUCE

4 large free-range egg yolks
1 tsp Dijon mustard
1 tsp dried tarragon
1 lemon, juiced and zested
125g salted butter
Pinch of black pepper

TO SERVE

4 brioche burger buns
1 handful of rocket leaves

HERE'S HOW:

Place the salmon into a food processor with the garlic, ginger, and parsley, then season with a little salt and pepper and blend until it forms a mince.

Using wet hands, shape the mixture into four equal portions and flatten into burgers.

Preheat a frying pan on a medium heat with a splash of oil and cook the burgers for 4 to 5 minutes on each side.

Meanwhile, to make the burger sauce, place the egg yolks into a bowl with the mustard, tarragon and the zest and juice of the lemon.

Heat the butter in the microwave until it is bubbling, then slowly pour it over the egg yolks, whisking continuously until it thickens and creates a sauce. Season with a little black pepper and set to one side.

When the burgers are cooked, place each one in a burger bun and top with rocket leaves and the tarragon burger sauce.

CHICKEN TIKKA BURGER

Prep time: 10 minutes, plus 30 minutes resting | Cooking time: 15 minutes | Serves 4

INGREDIENTS:

350g chicken breast, cubed
2 tbsp Indian Spice Mix (see page 176) or use shop-bought Indian spice mix
2 tbsp mango chutney
1 large free-range egg
50g dried breadcrumbs
Pinch of salt and pepper

TO SERVE
4 burger buns
4 tbsp mango chutney
8 tbsp Greek yoghurt
1 red onion, peeled and thinly sliced
2 handfuls of spinach leaves
1 handful of mint leaves, chopped
1 lemon, halved

HERE'S HOW:

Add the cubed chicken to a food processor with the spice mix, mango chutney, egg and breadcrumbs.

Season with a little salt and pepper before blending until smooth.

Divide into four portions (approx. 140g each), shape, and leave to rest for 30 minutes before cooking.

Cook the burgers in a preheated frying pan on a medium heat with a splash of olive oil. Fry for 6 to 8 minutes on each side or until fully cooked.

When the burgers are cooked, remove them from the pan and serve in burger buns with more mango chutney, Greek yoghurt, thinly sliced red onion and a few spinach leaves.

Finish with the chopped mint leaves and a squeeze of lemon before adding the top of the burger bun.

OXO BEEFY BURGER WITH CHIMICHURRI AND SWISS CHEESE

Prep time: 10 minutes | Cooking time: 10 minutes | Serves 4

INGREDIENTS:

300g good quality minced beef
100g sausage meat
40g butter, room temperature
1 OXO beef stock cube
1 tbsp olive oil
Pinch of salt and pepper

TO SERVE
4 slices of Swiss cheese
4 burger buns, lightly toasted
Chimichurri (see page 118)

HERE'S HOW:

Place the minced beef, sausage meat and butter into a mixing bowl.
Crumble the OXO cube over the meat before mixing it all together.

Using wet hands, divide into four equal portions and shape into burgers.

Season the burgers with olive oil, salt, and pepper, and cook in a nonstick pan on a medium heat for 4 to 5 minutes on each side.

When the burgers are cooked, lay a slice of Swiss cheese on top before serving in toasted buns with plenty of chimichurri salsa.

4 WAYS WITH FLAPJACK

Everybody loves a good homemade flapjack. I've taken my basic recipe and created four different combinations for you to try out. My favourite is the blueberry and pumpkin seed, but they're all tried, tested, and delicious.

MILLIONAIRES

Prep time: 15 minutes, plus 1 hour cooling | Cooking time: 40 minutes | Makes 9

INGREDIENTS:

FOR THE FLAPJACK BASE
225g salted butter or margarine

170g golden caster sugar

3 tbsp golden syrup

1 tbsp maple syrup

340g rolled oats

FOR THE CARAMEL
175g salted butter

175g golden caster sugar

4 tbsp golden syrup

397ml condensed milk

FOR THE TOPPING
200g dark chocolate

HERE'S HOW:

Preheat the oven to 170°c.

In a large pan, gently heat the butter or margarine, sugar, golden syrup and maple syrup. Heat until the butter has melted, then add the rolled oats and combine.

Spoon the mixture into a 20cm square baking tray lined with parchment paper.

Using the back of the spoon, press the flapjack down so it's even, then bake in the oven for 20 minutes.

Remove the tin from the oven and leave the flapjack to cool.

To make the caramel, place the butter, sugar, syrup and condensed milk into a saucepan and stir over a low heat until the butter has melted.

Turn the heat up and stir constantly for 5 minutes until the mixture becomes thick and fudge-like.

Pour the caramel over your cooked flapjack and leave to cool.

While your caramel is cooling, gently melt the chocolate before pouring it over the set caramel.

Leave to set fully before cutting.

CHIA AND ORANGE

Prep time: 15 minutes, plus 1 hour cooling | Cooking time: 25 minutes | Makes 9

INGREDIENTS:

250g unsalted butter

125g granulated sugar

125g light soft brown sugar

6 tbsp golden syrup

1 orange, juiced and zested

100g apricots, chopped

500g rolled oats

100g chia seeds

HERE'S HOW:

Preheat the oven to 170°c.

In a large pan, gently heat the butter, both sugars, golden syrup and orange zest until the butter has melted and the ingredients have combined.

Add the orange juice to a small pan with the chopped apricots, then turn to a high heat and switch off as soon as it reaches a boil. (We're not trying to cook anything here; we're just trying to get the orange flavour into the apricots so they become nice and plump).

Add the oats, chia seeds, apricots, and orange juice to the butter-sugar mixture and combine.

Spoon the mixture into a 20cm square baking tray lined with parchment paper.

Using the back of the spoon, press the flapjack down so it's even, then bake in the oven for 20 minutes.

Once baked, leave the flapjack to cool in the fridge for an hour before cutting.

BLUEBERRY AND PUMPKIN SEED

Prep time: 15 minutes, plus 1 hour cooling | Cooking time: 25 minutes | Makes 9

INGREDIENTS:

250g unsalted butter

125g granulated sugar

125g light soft brown sugar

6 tbsp golden syrup

1 lemon, juiced and zested

500g rolled oats

1 punnet of fresh blueberries (150g)

100g pumpkin seeds

HERE'S HOW:

Preheat the oven to 170°c.

In a large pan, gently heat the butter, both sugars, and the golden syrup until the butter has melted and the ingredients have combined.

Add the zest and juice of the lemon, then pour in the oats, blueberries and pumpkin seeds before stirring together to fully coat the oats.

Spoon the mixture into a 20cm square baking tray lined with parchment paper.

Using the back of the spoon, press the flapjack down so it's even, then bake in the oven for 20 minutes.

Once baked, leave the flapjack to cool in the fridge for an hour before cutting.

SEEDED WALNUT

Prep time: 15 minutes, plus 1 hour cooling | Cooking time: 25 minutes | Makes 9

INGREDIENTS:

250g unsalted butter

125g granulated sugar

125g light soft brown sugar

6 tbsp golden syrup

1 lemon, juiced and zested

500g rolled oats

150g California walnuts

100g mixed seeds

HERE'S HOW:

Preheat the oven to 170°c.

In a large pan, gently heat the butter, both sugars, and the golden syrup until the butter has melted and the ingredients have combined.

Add the zest and juice of the lemon, then pour in the oats, walnuts and mixed seeds before stirring together to fully coat the oats.

Spoon the mixture into a 20cm square baking tray lined with parchment paper.

Using the back of the spoon, press the flapjack down so it's even, then bake in the oven for 20 minutes.

Once baked, leave the flapjack to cool in the fridge for an hour before cutting.

4 WAYS WITH FRENCH ONION

French onion soup is a classic dish that originated in France in the 18th century. It's a hearty and flavourful soup made with onions, beef broth, bread, and cheese. The onions are typically sautéed until they are caramelised and then simmered in beef broth, giving the soup its rich and savoury flavour. The soup is usually served with a slice of toasted bread on top before being covered with melted cheese, usually Gruyère or Swiss. Here are some great ways to transform those delicious leftover onions (if you have any!).

FRENCH ONION SOUP

Prep time: 15 minutes | Cooking time: 50 minutes | Serves 4-6

INGREDIENTS:

4 medium white onions

1 tbsp olive oil

1 tsp salt

1 garlic bulb

150ml red wine

1 tbsp fresh thyme, chopped

1 tbsp fresh rosemary, chopped

1L beef stock (or vegetable stock)

HERE'S HOW:

Cut the onions in half and slice them as thinly as possible. This is important as it'll give great caramelisation when they cook.

Add the onions to a large pan with a splash of oil and salt. Cook on a medium heat for 15 to 20 minutes. (This sounds like a long time, but it'll really build the flavour and colour.)

While the onions are cooking, cut the top off the garlic bulb and add it to the pan. This will produce a nice, smooth flavour rather than a full-on garlic overload.

When the onions are soft, golden and caramelised, add the red wine and chopped herbs.

Bring to the boil and pour in the beef stock. Turn down to a simmer and leave on a gentle boil for 30 minutes until the liquid has reduced by half.

Taste the soup and season with salt and pepper if desired.

NOTE:

I like to serve the soup with a loaf of my sourdough bread as the heavy crust is perfect for dipping into the soup to soak up all that flavour.

FRENCH ONION BAGEL

Prep time: 45 minutes | Cooking time: 25 minutes | Makes 9

INGREDIENTS:

7g sachet of dried yeast

500g strong white bread flour

1 tsp dried onion powder

2 tbsp light soft brown sugar

150g cooked onions from the French Onion Soup, drained

1 tsp salt

1 tsp bicarbonate soda

1 free-range egg white, lightly beaten, for egg wash

70g parmesan

2 tbsp onion flakes

2 tbsp poppy seeds

HERE'S HOW:

Mix the dried yeast with 275ml water.

Put the flour, dried onion powder, sugar, cooked onions and a teaspoon of salt in a large bowl and mix to combine.

Add the yeasty liquid and mix into a rough dough.

Tip out onto a clean work surface and knead together until smooth and elastic – this should take around 10 minutes.

Put the dough into a lightly oiled bowl and cover with a piece of oiled cling film and leave to prove until it doubles in size.

Divide the dough into nine portions and form into balls (I like to weigh them first to make sure they're all the same size). Line the balls up on two parchment-lined baking trays and cover lightly with oiled cling film.

Leave for about 30 minutes or until risen and puffy, then remove the cling film.

Use a floured finger to make a hole in the centre of each bagel, swirling it around to stretch the dough a little, but being careful not to knock out too much air.

Preheat the oven to 160°c.

Fill a large saucepan with water and bring it to the boil. Add the bicarbonate of soda to alkalise the water.

Place two bagels in the water at a time and boil for 1 minute total (or 2 minutes if you prefer a chewier bagel), turning them over halfway through.

Using a slotted spoon, lift out the bagels, drain well, and return to the baking tray.

Brush the bagels with the beaten egg white and sprinkle with your topping of choice. (I like to use grated parmesan cheese, dried onion flakes, and poppy seeds.)

Bake for 20 to 25 mins or until golden-brown, then transfer to a wire rack to cool before eating.

NOTE:

These bagels will keep for three to four days or freeze for two months. Make sure to freeze in an airtight container to prevent freezer burn. I always slice my bagels before freezing so I can toast them straight from frozen.

FRENCH ONION TOAST

Cooking time: 10 minutes | Prep time: 5 minutes | Serves 2

INGREDIENTS:

1 large free-range egg yolk

1 tsp Dijon mustard

80g mature cheddar, grated

40g mozzarella, grated

20g parmesan, grated

1 tbsp chives, chopped

4 slices of crusty sourdough bread

15g butter, melted

60g cooked onions from the French Onion Soup, drained

HERE'S HOW:

If using, preheat the oven to 180°c.

Whisk the egg yolk and mustard together, then add all three grated cheeses and the chopped chives before stirring to combine.

Brush the melted butter onto one side of the bread, then place it butter side down on a baking tray. Repeat this step for all four slices.

Divide the cheese mixture between the bread, then top with the cooked onions.

Place the toasties into an oven or under a medium grill. They're ready to serve when the cheese is bubbling and melted.

FRENCH ONION PASTA

Prep time: 10 minutes | Cooking time: 15 minutes | Serves 2

INGREDIENTS:

180g dried spaghetti

1 tbsp extra-virgin olive oil, plus extra to serve

25g butter

1 clove of garlic, chopped

1 tsp fresh thyme, chopped

100g cooked onions from the French Onion Soup, drained

50g parmesan, grated

HERE'S HOW:

Cook the spaghetti in a large pot of salted water for 9 minutes, making sure to reserve some of the pasta water for later.

Meanwhile, preheat a large shallow pan and add the oil, butter, and chopped garlic.

Cook on a medium heat for 2 to 3 minutes, then add the chopped fresh thyme and cooked onions and stir together.

Spoon a ladle of pasta cooking water into the onions then turn the heat up and stir together.

When the spaghetti is cooked, use a pair of tongs to lift out the pasta and transfer it to the pan with the onions. Add half of the grated parmesan and stir together.

Serve the pasta in bowls and finish with a drizzle of extra-virgin olive oil for a nice, silky finish, then top with the remaining parmesan cheese.

4 WAYS WITH GNOCCHI

Gnocchi is one of my favourite things to make. Once you've made it fresh, the supermarket stuff will never seem the same again. It's surprisingly easy to make, and each of these flavour combinations makes the perfect midweek meal - all you've got to do is choose which to try first. Just remember: the key to perfect gnocchi is taking them all out when the first one rises to the top of the water. They'll overcook if you wait for them all to float!

FOR THE GNOCCHI

Prep time: 20 minutes | Cooking time: 1 hour | Serves 4 (100g per person)

INGREDIENTS:

300g potatoes (I recommend Maris Piper)
2 large free-range egg yolks
50g parmesan, grated
¼ tsp table salt
40g 00 pasta flour

HERE'S HOW:

Bake the potatoes in a preheated oven at 170°c for 1 hour or until soft on the inside and crisp on the outside.

When the potatoes are baked, remove them from the oven and cut them open on a chopping board – it's important to do this while they're hot as this will release all the steam and help make light and fluffy gnocchi.

Leave to cool for 5 minutes, then use a dessert spoon to scoop out all potatoes, leaving the skins, and use a masher or potato ricer to mash them until smooth.

Add the egg yolks, grated parmesan, and salt, then stir together.

Finally – and this step is really important – add the flour at the very end, as the less you work the flour, the better the gnocchi will be.

Once the flour is mixed in, the dough should stiffen up enough for you to transfer it to a lightly floured work surface and knead it gently for 20 seconds or so.

Cut the dough into four pieces and roll out each piece into a sausage shape. Then, cut each sausage into 2cm-wide pieces.

 Scan the QR Code to watch how to make this recipe

WALNUT AND MUSHROOM

Prep time: 10 minutes | Cooking time: 15 minutes | Serves 4

INGREDIENTS:

150g wild mushrooms

1 tbsp olive oil

1 tsp sea salt

1 clove of garlic

1 tsp fresh rosemary, chopped

1 tsp fresh thyme, chopped

50g butter

70g California walnuts

400g homemade gnocchi

80g parmesan, grated

HERE'S HOW:

Slice the mushrooms and place them into a pan with the oil and salt. Cook on a high heat for 6 to 7 minutes to draw out the natural moisture of the mushrooms, then evaporate the liquid to leave a delicious, meaty mushroom.

Once all the liquid has evaporated, add the garlic, chopped herbs and butter and continue to cook for another 2 minutes.

Scatter in the walnuts and stir together.

Cook the gnocchi in a large pan of salted boiling water for about 1 to 2 minutes. As soon as the first gnocchi rises to the top, use a slotted spoon to lift them all out of the water and into the sauce.

Gently stir the gnocchi and sauce together so as not to break up the gnocchi. Finish with grated parmesan and freshly milled black pepper.

TOMATO AND PECORINO

Prep time: 10 minutes | Cooking time: 15 minutes | Serves 4

INGREDIENTS:

1 medium white onion, cut into quarters

1 x 400g tin of good quality chopped tomatoes

Pinch of salt and pepper

50g butter

12 basil leaves

400g homemade gnocchi

Drizzle of extra-virgin olive oil

80g pecorino, grated

HERE'S HOW:

Place the quartered onion into a pan with the tinned tomatoes, salt, pepper, and butter.

Simmer for 10 to 15 minutes until the sauce is nice and rich.

Chop the basil with a sharp knife so as not to bruise the herb, then add it to the pan.

Stir together and taste for additional seasoning, if required.

Cook the gnocchi in a large pan of salted boiling water for about 1 to 2 minutes. As soon as the first gnocchi rises to the top, use a slotted spoon to lift them all out of the water and into the sauce.

Add a drizzle of extra-virgin olive oil to give a nice silkiness to the dish.

Gently stir the gnocchi and sauce together so as not to break up the gnocchi. Finish with the grated pecorino before serving.

PANCETTA AND GARLIC

Prep time: 5 minutes | Cooking time: 10 minutes | Serves 4

INGREDIENTS:

1 tbsp olive oil

3 cloves of garlic, chopped

100g pancetta

40g butter

1 tbsp fresh thyme, chopped

400g homemade gnocchi

40g parmesan, grated

Pinch of salt and pepper, to taste

HERE'S HOW:

Add the olive oil, garlic and pancetta to a large shallow frying pan and cook for 2 to 3 minutes, stirring until the pancetta is crispy, then add the butter and chopped thyme.

Cook the gnocchi in a large pan of salted boiling water for about 1 to 2 minutes. Add a ladle of the pasta cooking water to the garlic and pancetta to create an emulsion.

As soon as the first gnocchi rises to the top, use a slotted spoon to lift them all out of the water and into the sauce.

Add the grated parmesan into the frying pan and gently stir the gnocchi and sauce together so as not to break up the gnocchi. Season with salt and pepper to taste and serve.

LEMON AND RICOTTA

Prep time: 10 minutes | Cooking time: 10 minutes | Serves 4

INGREDIENTS:

2 tbsp olive oil

2 garlic cloves, sliced

25g butter

125g ricotta

1 tbsp lemon juice

70g parmesan, grated

400g homemade gnocchi

2 tbsp flat leaf parsley, chopped

Drizzle extra-virgin olive oil, to serve

Pinch of salt and pepper, to taste

HERE'S HOW:

Pour the olive oil into a large frying pan on a medium heat, then add the sliced garlic and butter and cook for 2 to 3 minutes. Turn the heat down and add the ricotta, lemon juice, and half of the parmesan cheese and stir together. Remove the pan from the heat and let the residual heat melt the ingredients.

Cook the gnocchi in a large pan of salted boiling water for about 1 to 2 minutes. As soon as the first gnocchi rises to the top, use a slotted spoon to lift them all out of the water and into the sauce.

Gently stir the gnocchi and sauce together so as not to break up the gnocchi. Finish with chopped parsley, the remaining parmesan cheese, and a drizzle of extra-virgin olive oil. Season with salt and pepper to taste and serve.

4 WAYS WITH HUMOUS

These days, humous is a weekly staple that most families enjoy. I thought it would be great to play around with some new flavour combinations to tickle your tastebuds. My favourite is the hazelnut and pomegranate humous - you get a burst of fruitness and a crunch from the hazelnuts in every dip!

BASIC HUMOUS

Prep time: 10 minutes | Serves 4

INGREDIENTS:

1 x 400g tin of chickpeas, drained
1 tbsp sesame paste
1 clove of garlic
1 lemon, juiced
275ml extra-virgin olive oil
3 tbsp water
Pinch of salt and pepper

HERE'S HOW:

Place the drained chickpeas, sesame paste, garlic, lemon juice, extra-virgin olive oil and water into a food processor.

Blend until smooth and season to taste with salt and pepper – it's your humous so adjust it to your taste!

PESTO HUMOUS

Prep time: 20 minutes | Serves 4

INGREDIENTS:

FOR THE PESTO

70g pine nuts

1 clove of garlic

1 tsp salt

1 large bunch of basil

30g parmesan, finely grated, plus more to serve

80ml extra-virgin olive oil

FOR THE HUMOUS

1 x 400g tin of chickpeas, drained

1 tbsp sesame paste

1 clove of garlic

1 lemon, juiced

275ml extra-virgin olive oil

3 tbsp water

Pinch of salt and pepper

HERE'S HOW:

To make the pesto, crush the pine nuts in a pestle and mortar, then add the garlic and salt and continue to grind.

Add the basil, continue to grind, then add the parmesan and oil.

Stir to combine and set to one side until you're ready to serve.

Place the drained chickpeas, sesame paste, garlic, lemon juice, extra-virgin olive oil and water into a food processor. Blend until smooth and season to taste.

Spread the humous on a plate, making waves with the back of a spoon. Add the pesto in and around the humous so that when you dip you get a little bit of both. Serve with extra grated parmesan on top.

HAZELNUT AND POMEGRANATE

Prep time: 10 minutes | Serves 4

INGREDIENTS:

1 x 400g tin of chickpeas, drained

1 tbsp sesame paste

100g Oregon hazelnuts

1 clove of garlic

1 lemon, juiced

275ml extra-virgin olive oil

3 tbsp water

Pinch of salt and pepper

2 tsp black and white sesame seeds

1 fresh pomegranate, cut in half and seeds removed

HERE'S HOW:

Place the drained chickpeas, sesame paste, hazelnuts, garlic, lemon juice, extra-virgin olive oil and water into a food processor. Blend until smooth and season to taste.

Spread the humous onto a plate and scatter over the sesame seeds. Finish with a sprinkling of pomegranate seeds and serve.

CARROT AND CUMIN SEED HUMOUS

Prep time: 10 minutes | Cooking time: 5 minutes | Serves 4

INGREDIENTS:

1 x 400g tin of chickpeas, drained

1 tbsp sesame paste

100g carrots, cooked

1 clove of garlic

1 handful of coriander (stalks for the humous; leaves for the topping)

1 lemon, juiced

275ml extra-virgin olive oil

3 tbsp water

Pinch of salt and pepper

3 tbsp olive oil

1 tbsp cumin seeds

HERE'S HOW:

Place the drained chickpeas, sesame paste, cooked carrots, garlic, coriander stalks, lemon juice, extra-virgin olive oil and water into a food processor. Blend until smooth and season to taste.

Heat the remaining oil in a frying pan and add the cumin seeds. As they heat, they will start to crackle – then, and only then, remove them from the heat.

Spread the humous onto a plate and scatter the hot cumin seeds and oil over the top, then finish with the fresh coriander leaves.

4 WAYS WITH INDIAN SPICE MIX

I love a bit of spice in my kitchen, and this combination results in absolute magic! These Indian-inspired flavours are warming, wonderful, and fragrant - just combine all the spices below and you'll have a versatile Indian Spice Mix that works wonders in so many dishes. Make more than you need and keep it stored in the cupboard. I guarantee you're going to want to use it more than once.

FOR THE INDIAN SPICE MIX

INGREDIENTS:

½ tsp chilli powder

1 tsp garam masala

2 tsp garlic powder

1 tsp ground coriander

1 tsp ground cumin

1 tsp ground ginger

1 tsp ground pepper

1 tsp paprika

1 tsp onion powder

1 tsp salt

2 tsp turmeric

BAKED CAULIFLOWER

Prep time: 40 minutes | Cooking time: 25 minutes | Serves 4

INGREDIENTS:

1 large head of cauliflower

2 tbsp salt

2 tbsp olive oil

3 tbsp Indian Spice Mix

200g baby spinach

HERE'S HOW:

Preheat the oven to 170°c.

Remove the outer green leaves from the cauliflower and cut it into small florets.

Place the cauliflower into a mixing bowl, season with salt, and leave for 30 minutes to draw a little of the moisture out.

Drian any excess water from the florets then add the olive oil and stir together.

Scatter over the spice mix, making sure all the cauliflower gets a dusting of the mix.

Spread the cauliflower onto a baking tray and cook in the oven for 25 minutes.

Once cooked, serve on a bed of baby spinach for a super tasty veggie meal.

MUSHROOM BIRIYANI PARCELS

Prep time: 10 minutes | Cooking time: 35 minutes | Serves 4

INGREDIENTS:

200g mushrooms, halved
2 olive oil
1 tsp salt
1 tbsp Indian Spice Mix
600g cooked rice
1 handful of fresh coriander leaf, chopped
1 lemon, halved
4 tbsp Oregon hazelnuts or almonds, sliced

HERE'S HOW:

If using, preheat the oven to 170°c.

Add the mushrooms to a nonstick frying pan on a medium heat and add a good splash of olive oil and a pinch of salt. The salt will draw out the moisture from the mushrooms and create a delicious flavour and texture.

Continue to cook the mushrooms to evaporate any liquid, then add the spice mix and remove from the heat.

Divide the cooked rice into four portions and place each one into the centre of a piece of parchment paper, approximately 30cm square.

Add some chopped coriander to each portion, then divide the mushrooms between each parcel of rice.

Add a squeeze of lemon juice and scatter over the nuts before folding up to create the parcels. Make sure to seal the edges to keep all the flavour and moisture inside.

Bake in the oven for 25 minutes, making sure the rice is nice and hot in the middle. You can even cook these in the microwave or air fryer — just heat until fully warmed through.

SPICED CHICKEN

Prep time: 10 minutes, plus 1 hour marinating | Cooking time: 25-45 minutes | Serves 4

INGREDIENTS:

4 chicken legs, on the bone
4 chicken thighs, on the bone
4 chicken wings
4 tbsp Indian Spice Mix
4 tbsp Greek yoghurt
Drizzle of olive oil

HERE'S HOW:

Using a sharp knife, make four to five cuts down to the bone in each piece of chicken (this will help get plenty of flavour into the chicken and speed up the cooking process).

Put the chicken into a mixing bowl with the spice mix and yoghurt. Get your hands into the bowl and combine so the chicken is fully coated, ensuring you get the marinade into the cuts so you get in lots of flavour.

Cover the chicken and leave to marinate for 1 hour (or overnight if you prefer).

When ready to cook, place the chicken onto a shallow baking tray and drizzle with a little olive oil.

Season with salt and then cook in a preheated oven at 170°c for 45 minutes. If you want to use the air fryer, cook at 170°c for 25 minutes.

LAMB TRAYBAKE

Prep time: 20 minutes | Cooking time: 25-45 minutes | Serves 4

INGREDIENTS:

6 lamb chops
3 tbsp olive oil
2 tbsp Indian Spice Mix
Pinch of salt and pepper
1 sweet potato, peeled and chopped in quarters
½ butternut squash peeled and cut into 1cm thick pieces
2 red onions, cut into sixths
150g California prunes
½ pomegranate, seeds removed
2 tbsp fresh coriander leaf

HERE'S HOW:

Preheat the oven to 170°c.

Place the lamb chops into a mixing bowl with the olive oil and spice mix.

Using your hands, rub the oil and spice into the lamb to help get a nice even flavour all the way round the meat. Set the bowl to one side.

Place the sweet potato, squash and red onions into a mixing bowl with a splash of olive oil and a good pinch of salt and pepper.

Mix with your hands to coat the vegetables, then turn the bowl out onto a large baking tray.

Cook the vegetables in the oven for 30 minutes or until just tender, then remove the tray and lay the lamb chops on top of the veggies.

Scatter over the prunes and return to the oven for 15 minutes for juicy pink lamb chops. If you prefer your lamb more well done, continue cooking for an additional 5 to 10 minutes.

If cooking in the air fryer, cook the veggies for 15 minutes at 180°c, then add the lamb and prunes and cook for a further 10 minutes.

Once cooked to your preference, finish with pomegranate seeds and fresh coriander leaf.

4 WAYS WITH PESTO

Fresh pesto is a family favourite in most homes these days, but it doesn't always have to be a classic basil pesto. Here are four different ways to experiment with pesto.

WALNUT PESTO

Prep time: 10 minutes | Cooking time: 10 minutes | Serves 4

INGREDIENTS:

400g dried spaghetti
200g California walnuts
1 clove of garlic
1 tsp sea salt
½ lemon, juiced
80ml extra-virgin olive oil
45g parmesan, grated, plus extra to serve

HERE'S HOW:

Cook the pasta in salted boiling water for 9 minutes, making sure to reserve some of the pasta water to loosen the sauce later.

Meanwhile, place the remaining ingredients into a food processor and blend until smooth.

Taste your pesto and season with a little salt and pepper if required.

Add a couple of spoonfuls of pasta water to the pesto to create a loose sauce, then add to the spaghetti and stir to coat.

Finish with extra grated parmesan and serve.

Scan the QR Code to watch how to make this recipe

HAZELNUT AND BASIL PESTO

Prep time: 10 minutes | Cooking time: 10 minutes | Serves 4

INGREDIENTS:

400g dried spaghetti

70g roasted Oregon hazelnuts, plus extra
to serve

1 large bunch of fresh basil

1 clove of garlic

1 tsp salt

80ml extra-virgin olive oil

½ lemon, juiced

30g parmesan, grated, plus extra to serve

HERE'S HOW:

Cook the pasta in salted boiling water for 9 minutes, making sure to
reserve some of the pasta water to loosen the sauce later.

Meanwhile, place the remaining ingredients into a food processor and
blend until smooth.

Taste your pesto and season with a little salt and pepper if required.

Add a couple of spoonfuls of pasta water to the pesto to create a loose
sauce, then add to the spaghetti and stir to coat.

Finish with grated parmesan and a few chopped hazelnuts for added
crunch.

MUSHROOM PESTO

Prep time: 15 minutes | Cooking time: 20 minutes | Serves 4

INGREDIENTS:

225g chestnut mushrooms, sliced

½ tsp sea salt

400g dried spaghetti

30g dried porcini mushrooms, soaked in boiling water and drained

50g California walnuts

1 clove of garlic

1 tsp fresh thyme

1 tsp fresh rosemary

100ml extra-virgin olive oil

70g parmesan, freshly grated, plus extra to serve

HERE'S HOW:

Add the chestnut mushrooms and salt to a pan and fry for 10 minutes. Adding the salt helps to evaporate all the moisture from the mushrooms and give them a great texture.

Cook the pasta in salted boiling water for 9 minutes, making sure to reserve some of the pasta water to loosen the sauce later.

Meanwhile, place the remaining ingredients and the cooked chestnut mushrooms into a food processor and blend until smooth.

Taste your pesto and season with a little salt and pepper if required.

Add a couple of spoonfuls of pasta water to the pesto to create a loose sauce, then add to the spaghetti and stir to coat.

Finish with extra grated parmesan and serve.

SPINACH AND FETA PESTO

Prep time: 10 minutes | Cooking time: 10 minutes | Serves 4

INGREDIENTS:

400g dried spaghetti

300g fresh spinach

80g salted peanuts

50g parmesan or pecorino cheese, grated

1 clove of garlic

80ml extra-virgin olive oil

½ lemon, juiced

½ slice of bread

40g feta (20g in the pesto; 20g to serve)

HERE'S HOW:

Cook the pasta in salted boiling water for 9 minutes, making sure to reserve some of the pasta water to loosen the sauce later.

Meanwhile, place the remaining ingredients into a food processor and blend until smooth.

Taste your pesto and season with a little salt and pepper if required.

Add a couple of spoonfuls of pasta water to the pesto to create a loose sauce, then add to the spaghetti and stir to coat.

Finish with a sprinkle of the remaining feta and serve.

4 WAYS WITH PIZZA

Cooking pizza at home is not as difficult as you think - you just need to make sure you don't bite off more than you can chew! Try making and cooking your pizzas one at a time as domestic ovens aren't designed to cook all the pizzas at once. Each one of these recipes is for four pizzas, but you can mix and match toppings to your liking.

PIZZA DOUGH

Prep time: 20 minutes, plus 4-6 hours proving | Makes 4 pizzas

INGREDIENTS:

500g white bread flour

7g dried yeast

1 tsp fine sea salt

2 tbsp extra-virgin olive oil

325ml water

4 tbsp ground polenta or corn, for rolling

4 tbsp plain flour, for rolling

HERE'S HOW:

Place the flour into a mixing bowl with the dried yeast and salt and use your hand to blend it together.

Make a well in the middle and pour in the oil and water. Then, use one hand in a claw shape to roll it around the bowl and form a ball of dough.

Transfer the dough onto a clean, lightly floured work surface before kneading for 5 to 10 minutes until smooth and stretchy. Return the dough to the mixing bowl, cover, and leave to prove for 2 to 3 hours.

Once the dough has doubled in size, scoop it out onto a clean work surface and divide it into four equal portions.

Evenly space out the balls of dough on a baking tray dusted with a little flour and ground polenta to ensure they don't stick together when they prove, then cover them with a clean tea towel. Leave to prove in the fridge for 2 to 3 hours before baking to develop the flavour as much as possible.

When ready to bake, roll out the balls of dough, using the polenta and flour to dust the worktop, and place the pizza bases onto floured baking sheets ready for topping.

PIZZA BIANCO

Prep time: 10 minutes | Cooking time: 15 minutes | Makes 4 pizzas

INGREDIENTS:

250g mascarpone cream

4 tbsp extra-virgin olive oil

2 red chillies, finely diced

2 tbsp mini capers, chopped

8 slices Parma ham

Fennel tops (optional)

HERE'S HOW:

Preheat the oven to 200°c.

Spoon the mascarpone onto the pizza bases - about five to six small spoons of mascarpone per pizza.

Pour over a drizzle of olive oil and scatter with the freshly chopped chilli and capers.

Lay the Parma ham on top of the pizza and season with a little black pepper, then repeat the process until you have topped all the pizzas.

Bake for 12 to 15 minutes or until golden, then finish the pizza with a scattering of fresh fennel tops for a beautiful, fresh flavour.

HERITAGE TOMATO AND BURRATA

Prep time: 15 minutes | Cooking time: 15 minutes | Makes 4 pizzas

INGREDIENTS:

FOR THE BASE

1 x 400g tin of good quality chopped tomatoes

1 clove of garlic, finely chopped

1 tsp dried oregano

1 tbsp olive oil

½ tsp salt

FOR THE TOPPING

300g heritage tomatoes, halved

1 tbsp balsamic vinegar

1 tsp honey

2 tbsp extra-virgin olive oil

Pinch of salt and pepper, to taste

1 handful of fresh basil

4 burrata (1 per pizza)

HERE'S HOW:

Preheat the oven to 200°c.

To make the sauce, pop the tomatoes into a sieve and drain the excess liquid.

Place the drained tomatoes and remaining base ingredients into a clean bowl and combine.

Divide the sauce between the pizza bases and spread evenly.

For the topping, add the heritage tomatoes to a bowl along with the vinegar, honey, olive oil, salt and pepper, then distribute them over the pizzas.

Bake for 12 to 15 minutes or until golden.

To finish the pizza, scatter over the fresh basil leaves and place a burrata in the centre of each pizza. Drizzle with a little extra olive oil, sprinkle with black pepper, and serve.

WILD MUSHROOM AND TALEGGIO

Prep time: 15 minutes | Cooking time: 25 minutes | Makes 4 pizzas

INGREDIENTS:

FOR THE BASE

1 x 400g tin of good quality chopped tomatoes

1 clove of garlic, finely chopped

1 tsp dried oregano

1 tbsp olive oil

½ tsp salt

FOR THE TOPPING

200g wild mushroom, sliced

1 tsp salt

1 tbsp rosemary, chopped

1 tbsp olive oil

200g taleggio cheese

HERE'S HOW:

Preheat the oven to 200°c.

To make the sauce, pop the tomatoes in a sieve and drain the excess liquid.

Place the drained tomatoes and remaining base ingredients into a clean bowl and combine.

Preheat a shallow frying pan on medium heat and add the mushrooms, salt, rosemary and olive oil. Cook for 10 minutes until all the moisture has evaporated - this is the secret to making mushrooms taste amazing!

Divide the sauce between the pizza bases and spread evenly, then scatter the mushrooms on top of the pizza sauce and divide the cheese between each.

Bake for 12 to 15 minutes or until golden.

PEPPERONI WITH SPICY HONEY

Prep time: 15 minutes | Cooking time: 20 minutes | Makes 4 pizzas

INGREDIENTS:

FOR THE BASE

1 x 400g tin of good quality chopped tomatoes

1 clove of garlic, finely chopped

1 tsp dried oregano

1 tbsp olive oil

½ tsp salt

FOR THE TOPPING

4 tbsp honey

1 red chilli, finely chopped

100g sliced pepperoni

225g fresh mozzarella balls

1 handful of fresh basil

HERE'S HOW:

Preheat the oven to 200°c.

To make the sauce, pop the tomatoes in a sieve and drain the excess liquid.

Place the drained tomatoes and remaining base ingredients into a clean bowl and combine.

Place the honey and chilli into a saucepan and warm gently for 2 to 3 minutes.

Divide the sauce and pepperoni between the pizza bases and distribute evenly.

Cut the mozzarella balls in half and squeeze out the excess liquid, then tear them up into pieces and place them on the pizzas.

Season with a little black pepper and bake for 12 to 15 minutes or until golden.

Once the pizzas are baked, drizzle with the chilli honey and finish with fresh basil leaves.

CONVERSION CHARTS

WEIGHTS

25g – 1 oz

50g – 2 oz

100g – 3½ oz

150g – 5 oz

200g – 7 oz

250g – 9 oz

275g – 10 oz

500g – 1 lb 2 oz

LIQUIDS

5ml – 1 tsp

15ml – 1 tbsp

30ml – ⅛ cup

60ml – ¼ cup

75ml – ⅓ cup

125ml – ½ cup

150ml – ⅔ cup

175ml – ¾ cup

250ml – 1 cup

OVEN TEMPERATURES
(CELSIUS TO FAHRENHEIT)

140°c – 275°F

150°c – 300°F

170°c – 325°F

180°c – 350°F

190°c – 375°F

200°c – 400°F

220°c – 425°F

OTHER APPROXIMATE MEASURES

Grated Cheese: 1 cup = 100g

Uncooked Pasta: 1 cup = 100g

Uncooked Rice: 1 cup = 200g

TAYLOR
1476
1 1/2 tbsp | 22.5ml
1 tbsp | 15ml
1 tsp | 5ml
1/2 tsp | 2.5ml
1/4 tsp | 1.25ml
1/8 tsp | 0.65ml